JUST IN TIME!

HEALING SERVICES

James K. Wagner

Abingdon Press
Nashville

JUST IN TIME!
HEALING SERVICES

This book is printed on acid-free paper.

Library of Congress Cataloging-in-Publication Data

Wagner, James K.
    Healing services / James K. Wagner.
        p. cm. — (Just in time! ; 5)
    Includes bibliographical references and indexes.
    ISBN 978-0-687-64248-9 (binding: pbk.,adhesive perfect : alk. paper)
        1. Spiritual healing. 2. Healing—Religious aspects—Christianity. I. Title.
    BT732.5.W335 2007
    265'.82—dc22

                                                                        2006103254

07 08 09 10 11 12 13 14 15 16—10 9 8 7 6 5 4 3 2 1
MANUFACTURED IN THE UNITED STATES OF AMERICA

To all who seek health and wholeness in body,

mind, spirit, and relationships so freely offered by

the compassionate, loving, healing Christ

A Prayer for the Guidance of the Holy Spirit

Come, Holy Spirit, enlighten my mind, cleanse my motives,
    clarify my intentions and guide my ambitions,
    especially in this matter and mystery of healing.

When full understanding is not possible,
    give me faith to trust in you anyway.
When my questions are greater than my answers,
    give me faith to trust in you anyway.
When my doubts outweigh my certainties,
    give me faith to trust in you anyway.

Above all else, Holy Spirit of the Living God,
    decrease my desire to live in my restrictive world of self and
    increase my desire to live in the freedom of your Kingdom.

In the name of the One who makes possible the answer to this
        prayer,
    in the name of Jesus, I offer this request. Amen.

—James K. Wagner, Introduction to *Letters on the Healing Ministry*

CONTENTS

INTRODUCTION

Those who design and lead worship will discover in this book guidelines and resources for healing ministry that is Christ-centered and can be adapted in a variety of settings. Although God uses medicine, hospitals, and various remedies in the healing process, these avenues for improving health do not address the spiritual heart of humankind. Does this imply that local churches might replace local hospitals? Not at all! The churches, however, can offer spiritual therapy not provided by health care professionals. God, as revealed in Jesus Christ—who is loving, compassionate, and on the side of good health—intends for us to seek and use the best medical care and the best spiritual care combined. Consider these ten reasons why the church is uniquely qualified as a primary healing community. The church:

1. Presents all of Christ's ministries: teaching, preaching, and healing;
2. Engages in whole person healing (body, mind, spirit, relationships);
3. Encourages a lifestyle of prayer;
4. Emphasizes the role of faith;
5. Deals with the root causes of illnesses;
6. Is an extended family giving care, love, and support;
7. Practices one-on-one ministry;
8. Cooperates with health care professionals;
9. Advocates and promotes the health of our natural environment;
10. Offers spiritual therapies, such as the sacraments, prayer and meditation, biblical insights and values, forgiveness, worship opportunities, spiritual companionship, and the healing Christ.

During his earthly ministry Jesus clearly understood and demonstrated the interrelatedness between physical, mental, and spiritual health, as well as healthy relationships. Because Jesus loved the whole person, his goal was to help each person become whole and healthy. This is also the mission of the church. Those who take leadership in this ministry need to be holistic and comprehend the wide range of healing possibilities. Defining health as the absence of disease is too narrow. The noted author, minister, and pioneer in healing ministry Albert E. Day reminds us that health is "the combination of harmonious relationships, spiritual vitality, psychological maturity, and physical wellness" (Albert E. Day, *Letters on the Healing Ministry*, 7–8).

Ponder this statement in the *United Methodist Book of Worship*:

> A Service of Healing is not necessarily a service of curing, but it provides an atmosphere in which healing can happen. The greatest healing of all is the reunion or reconciliation of a human being with God. When this happens, physical healing sometimes occurs, mental and emotional balance is often restored, spiritual health is enhanced, and relationships are healed. For the Christian the basic purpose of spiritual healing is to renew and strengthen one's relationship with the living Christ. (613–14)

Whether you are new to this ministry or an experienced leader, the author recommends that those who use this resource first read each chapter to get a grasp of what this book provides. Chapter 1 deals with frequently asked questions and could be used in teaching opportunities and with small group studies. Chapter 2 presents several tested practices that are effective in developing and offering a public healing service. Chapters 3 through 14 offer a variety of healing services, formats, and liturgies that could be used in traditional church settings, as well as outside the church for special needs and occasions. A mini-concordance of all the New Testament healing stories, plus some recorded in the Old Testament, are listed in an appendix: Biblical Healing Passages. For quick cross-references see the Scripture Index, the Music Index, and the Communion Liturgy Index. Selected Resources are for those who want to research and study more comprehensively the healing ministry of Christ in the church today.

The services you will find in this book could be called "Liturgies for Healing Services." The word "liturgy" comes from the Greek and means "the work of the people." Whenever and wherever Christians assemble for worship, patterns emerge that are designed to assist the worshipers in connecting with God. Our worshipful work, what we bring and what we do in worship, is our gift to God; what God brings and does for us in worship is God's gift to us.

Careful and prayerful planning is required for effective healing ministry. The order of the service (the liturgy), the physical surroundings, and the hospitable, sensitively caring attitude of the worship leaders work together in creating an environment for God's healing to happen. Healing services can be offered at the church on a regular basis, as well as in times of emergency and crisis situations. Healing services can also be held outside the church building in a variety of settings such as small group ministries, home and hospital visitation, church camps, spiritual retreats, retirement and nursing centers, seminars and workshops, convocations and conferences.

Some of these healing services are ready to use as printed, with step-by-step suggestions. Words in bold print, in prayers and liturgies, are meant to be said in unison by the whole congregation. Words in regular print are meant to be said by one person, the presider, or pastor. Directions are occaisonally given in italic print. Others are in outline form awaiting the worship planners' creativity. Whatever format you choose, be attentive to the setting and to the particular needs of the participants. Be compassionate. Be flexible. Be faithful. Be obedient to the Healing Christ. Be open to the discernment and guidance of the Holy Spirit.

A CHALLENGE AND A CAUTION

This appropriate word of challenge and caution comes from the heart and spirit of Albert E. Day (1884–1973), a minister who conducted weekly healing services as a Methodist pastor in the 1940s and 1950s. Dr. Day was also the founder and guiding force behind the Disciplined Order of Christ, an ecumenical spiritual renewal movement. The following is reprinted from his excellent book, *Letters on the Healing Ministry*:

> Blessings on you who are seeking to follow in the footsteps of Jesus and to fulfill his command to heal the sick in his name and through his name and through his power. Keep humble. Hold sacred the confidences entrusted to your keeping. Be patient with those who need to come again and again. Guard against the intrusions of well-meaning people who have an unenlightened zeal for God and whose too readily volunteered testimony and exhortation are the source of endless confusion. Let no current skepticisms daunt you. Not everyone will experience the specific healing he or she is seeking, but many will. However, each one will be blessed and helped in some way. Be alert to discover in the unhealed or in their environment or in yourself any hindrances to the renewal of life and seek to clear them away. This ministry requires constant self-examination and ever larger dedication. Whatever else you do, keep on loving those who need you, those who oppose you, those who fail you. If necessary, lose your life for their sakes and for Christ. So doing you will find life for yourself and for your people on deeper levels. You are Christ's missioner and he will never fail you or your people! (Albert Day, *Letters on the Healing Ministry* [Methodist Evangelist Materials, revised edition published by Upper Room Books, 1986], 130. Used by permission of the Disciplined Order of Christ.)

CHAPTER ONE

QUESTIONS ABOUT HEALING MINISTRY

1. WHY HAVE A HEALING SERVICE?

Some may say, "Should not every worship service be a healing experience? What is the point of having a special healing service?" Although it is true that whenever two or three or more gather in the name of Jesus Christ many good things happen, the average Sunday morning worship service does not focus specifically on healing. Just as we have special emphasis on evangelism, music, stewardship, education, missions, and social concerns, we need to have specific times to center on healing ministry. When Jesus sent out his disciples two by two (Luke 9:1-2), he commanded them to heal in his name. This directive from Jesus was meant not only for the early church, but also for the church today (John 14:12-14). Regularly scheduled healing services proclaim to the congregation and to the surrounding community that God is on the side of good health and welcomes all who seek help, hope, and healing.

2. WHAT TO CALL THIS MINISTRY?

This significant ministry goes by several labels: faith healing, divine healing, spiritual healing, and Christian healing. Because each of these names can be widely or narrowly interpreted, the preferred designation by many is simply, "The Healing Ministry of Christ." Whatever you call this health-enhancing, vital ministry; you will need to provide educational settings for clarification, understanding, and acceptance. Teaching ministry and healing ministry go together.

3. What Is Christ-centered Healing Ministry?

Christians do not have a monopoly on healing. God loves and cares for the whole world, Christians and non-Christians alike. God has unlimited avenues for healing, many ways of curing the illnesses of humankind. Health care professionals, religious as well as nonreligious, are engaged in various aspects of healing ministry even though God's grace and benevolence may not be acknowledged. What is unique for Christians in the healing process is the presence and power of the risen Christ, who not only instructed his followers after Easter to continue all of his ministries (teaching, preaching, healing), but he also promised, "Remember, I am with you always, to the end of the age" (Matthew 28:18-20). Healing ministry is not magic, sleight of hand, or hocus-pocus.

Rather, it is biblically based, holistic in scope, and Christ-centered. By genuine acts of faith and confidence Christians affirm and call on Christ-the-Healer to do the healing ministry through us, in us, and among us.

4. Is Healing Ministry a Substitute for Medicine?

Although healing ministry often results in restored physical health, this is not a substitute for medicine or surgery. Healing ministry makes no claims to prescribe in the arenas of psychology, psychiatry, medical procedures, and medicine, but does work closely with persons in these professions. Increasing numbers in the medical community realize and appreciate the therapeutic value of religious faith. God uses countless ways of providing good health. As a medical doctor said so well, "God is our primary physician and all the doctors on earth are junior partners." Combining the best spiritual care with the best medical care is highly recommended.

5. What Is Meant by Healing Prayer?

Healing prayer means using prayer as a spiritual therapy in healing the whole person (body, mind, spirit, and relationships). Those who pray take seriously the spiritual dimension in the healing process. Out of obedience to Christ and compassion for others intentional prayers for healing can be incorporated into the life of every church. Intercessory prayer groups are on the front line in healing ministry. Any expansion of prayer ministries within the local church provides the necessary foundation for effective healing ministries. Prayer ministry is healing ministry; healing ministry is prayer ministry. However, keep in mind that prayer does not heal; prayer connects us with God, the source of health and wholeness. When we pray for healing, we are not in a begging posture; rather we are coming to God with an attitude of cooperation, gratitude and receptivity in the healing process.

6. Who Are the People Who Serve on Prayer Teams?

The healing ministry instructions recorded in James 5:14 direct those who are ill to "call for the elders of the church and have them pray over them, anointing them with oil in the name of the Lord." The term "elders" literally means "church leaders." One interpretation suggests that the elders are those Christians who give evidence of personal growth in the mind and spirit of Christ. Lay and clergy members of the church community who believe that Christ is alive and able to touch, help, and heal today just as in the New Testament era, volunteer to serve on prayer teams. These spiritual leaders have no special power or healing ability, but combine their personal faith in the healing Christ with a genuine compassion for people. Any healing that occurs comes by way of the love and grace of God in Christ.

7. WHAT IS THE ROLE OF FAITH IN HEALING?

Faith is critical in healing; however, having faith in faith is not helpful. What counts is placing one's personal trust, belief, and faith in God, our Divine Physician. A close examination of every healing story of Jesus in the four gospels reveals that faith in God to heal is present in someone. The faith of the person seeking help is not always known, but Jesus consistently manifests faith. Medical research in our day is demonstrating the positive effects of faith in God, especially during surgical procedures and life-threatening illnesses. The role of faith is crucial; and the more we exercise our personal faith in God, who cares and heals, the better the results.

8. ARE SPIRITUAL GIFTS NECESSARY FOR HEALING MINISTRY?

The Holy Spirit endows all Christians with gifts for ministry. The New Testament names at least twenty different spiritual gifts. Christians are encouraged to discover and use their various gifts in building up the Body of Christ. However, gifts of healing

(1 Corinthians 12:9) are not a requirement for effective healing ministry. Gifts of healing are a plus but not a prerequisite. The healing ministry of the church is primarily a ministry of obedience to Christ and of compassion for people. Underline and remember this affirmation by a Presbyterian minister who has had many years of experience conducting healing services: "It is not our ability but our availability that is desired. Jesus Christ will do the work and supply the power" (Donald Bartow, *The Healing Service* [Canton, Ohio: Life Enrichment Publishers, 1976], 15).

9. WHAT IS THE SIGNIFICANCE OF ANOINTING WITH OIL?

In the Bible, oil was at times used as a medicinal agent (Isaiah 1:6 and Luke 10:34). Jesus instructed the disciples to anoint with oil when they prayed for healing, as recorded in Mark 6:13. The often-quoted instructions in James 5:13-16 are quite clear in calling the spiritual leaders of the church to pray with the sick and anoint them with oil in the name of the Lord. The oil does not do the healing; rather, being anointed with oil reminds us of the healing presence of Christ. Today Christians interpret anointing with oil as an authentic biblical symbol for healing ministry.

10. WHY LAY ON HANDS IN HEALING MINISTRY?

"The early Christians employed the laying on of hands in . . . ordination [ceremonies], in the commissioning of missionaries, in receiving the baptism of the Holy Spirit, and in healing" ministry. "According to the Gospel records, Jesus did not hesitate to use physical touch in communicating God's love . . . when he sensed that would be appropriate . . . Because of the obvious biblical precedent, coupled with our natural desire to reach out to people in need, we should not hesitate to touch gently and lovingly those who ask for healing prayer with laying on of hands" (Wagner, *An Adventure in Healing and Wholeness*, 98, 97, and 99).

11. WHEN HEALING DOES NOT HAPPEN, THEN WHAT?

This frequently raised question usually indicates the disappointment of not being healed physically. What some might label as failure in healing ministry often disregards spiritual health, mental/emotional health, and healthy relationships. Although a specific cure may not happen, other kinds of healings can be experienced. Actually, there are no total failures and absolute disappointments according to those who actively participate in healing ministry. All are blessed in helpful ways. Hope replaces fear. Resentments melt away. Worry is vanquished. Sins are forgiven. Guilt is erased. Broken lives are mended. The inner peace of God is present. When improved physical health is not experienced, for whatever reason, God is faithful and blesses us in other areas of our life and being.

12. AFTER RECEIVING PRAYERS FOR HEALING, WHAT SHOULD I EXPECT?

Just relax and give God time to work. When we plant a garden we do not pull up our seedlings every day to see how much they have grown. Adopt this same attitude with spiritual therapy. Sometimes prayers for healing are answered very quickly and sometimes quite gradually. God's health care plan is to heal the whole person, not just the part that hurts. If we become impatient with the healing process, remember that our timing is not always the same as God's. Our role is to remain faithful, patient, and fully trusting in God's good will for health and wholeness.

CHAPTER TWO

DEVELOPING THE PUBLIC HEALING SERVICE

The purpose of a public healing service is to present the total ministry of Jesus Christ, teaching, preaching, and with an intentional focus on healing:

- The healing of the body, the mind, and the spirit.
- The healing of attitudes and emotions that builds healthy relationships between persons, families, churches, cultures, races, and nations.
- The healing of brokenness wherever it is encountered in life.

The mood is one of sincere worship and prayerful expectancy. At a healing service each worshiper is made aware of God's love and forgiveness, acceptance and pardon, wholeness and salvation, peace and joy, encouragement and hope. The focal point is the life and ministry of Jesus Christ. When people experience Christ's presence in their lives, healing and wholeness happen on several levels. The statement has been made that evangelism and healing ministries are closely related.

Prior to announcing the first public healing service, the pastor needs to inform the congregation about her or his interest in the healing ministry. Crucial in the preparation stage is the discovery of those church members who also have openness to this ministry. Sermon series based on the healing stories of Jesus, pastoral articles in the church newsletter, informal conversations, and short-term, small group study opportunities are some of the ways to promote dialog and communication.

Healing ministry that is primarily initiated, organized, and solely led by the pastor will have limited influence in the ongoing life of the congregation. Lay leadership must be involved in every facet of healing ministry. The wise pastor will offer training and leadership opportunities for motivated, concerned, and talented laypersons.

Consider taking an experimental approach to the scheduling of healing services. Set a time limit and establish ways to evaluate the experiment. Congregational governing bodies and official boards are more likely to cooperate on this basis. Set an initial time frame of three to four months with the assurance that evaluations will be made and reported. Toward the end of the experimental period, return to the policy-making body of the church with reportable data and specific recommendations. The following questionnaire (adapted from Wagner, *An Adventure in Healing and Wholeness*, 133–34) provides one format for gathering feedback.

QUESTIONNAIRE RELATED TO CHURCH HEALING SERVICES

1. I have attended regularly_____ occasionally_____ once_____
2. I think the healing services should be continued:
   Yes___ No___
3. I like the present time of the services: Yes___ No___
4. I could attend more often if these services were held at another time: Yes___ No___

5. Here are my suggestions for different times to offer the healing services:
6. The parts of the service I like best are:
7. The parts of the service I like the least are:
8. I personally have been helped by this healing ministry:
   ___ Spiritually
   ___ Emotionally
   ___ Physically
   ___ Relationships with others
   ___ Other ways (please be specific)
9. Suggestions for improving the effectiveness of these services:

   _____

   _____

10. I am interested in attending a short-term study course or a one-day seminar dealing with an in-depth look at the healing ministry of Christ in the church today:
    Yes____ No____
11. Personal comments and questions:

Signature (optional) _____

Please return this questionnaire to the church office by _____(date). Thank you for your assistance in evaluating this ministry.

CONSIDERATIONS AND ACTION

(The following is adapted from Wagner, An Adventure in Healing and Wholeness, *130–32.)*

After deciding to begin, other questions arise for consideration and action:

- Should the healing services be formal or informal?
- How frequently should we offer these services? Weekly or monthly?

- What day and hour should we hold these services?
- Should we have Holy Communion, anointing oil, and a printed order of service?
- What about appropriate music?
- What room in the church to use?
- Who will lead the services?
- Who shall we invite to be on the prayer teams?

Begin with the familiar. Don't try to copy a worship style that is radically different from your own. Design a basic liturgy that participants can understand and accept.

It is always helpful, especially in the early stages, to explain to those who gather for healing what you are doing and why you are doing it. Teaching moments can be presented twenty or thirty minutes before the healing service begins, introduced with each part of the service, or incorporated in a homily. The goal is to put the worshipers "at ease," not to foster "dis-ease" in the healing environment.

Attendance at local church healing services often falls below the expectation level of the persons in charge. Regardless of the size of the church, attendance will likely be a small group. However, our goal and purpose is to be faithful and obedient to Christ in offering a regular, well-publicized time for all interested persons to participate in healing ministry opportunities. Some will be there every time; others only when they are facing a crisis. Many who do not attend will submit prayer requests. Remember that the healing Christ can use the faith, love, compassion, and prayers of a few to feed the multitude. An ounce of obedience is worth a ton of Bible study.

When Praying with Others

Someone has rightly said that those who desire to be creative must stay close to the Creator. Likewise, those who are invited or called into a ministry of healing must stay close to the Healer. Praying with and for others is nothing less than a high and holy privilege. Whether you serve on a prayer team or pray one-with-one, prepare yourself by giving thanks to God for allowing you to serve in Christ's ministry of healing and wholeness. Your part in praying with people is to be a compassionate, caring friend, an instrument for Christ's love to flow, to touch, to heal.

Sometimes praying with others is compared to serving the bread and the cup in Holy Communion. Christians come to the Lord's Table not to get in touch with those who serve, but rather to be touched by the Lord Jesus Christ. The communion servers have an important but secondary role. So it is in prayers for healing. Those who pray with and for others have a secondary role. They assist people in staying connected or in reconnecting with the Healing Christ. Those who serve on prayer teams are not responsible for solving problems or curing illnesses. That is the unique function and character of Christ, who promised to be with us always and in all that we do (Matthew 28:20).

"When praying with others [for healing and wholeness], it is not necessary to 'work up a sweat'" (Wagner, *An Adventure in Healing and Wholeness,* 139). We are not in a begging posture; rather, we are giving God an opportunity to be active and directive in our personal situations. God respects human free will and always welcomes our receptivity to spiritual help and healing. Our prayers are acts of personal cooperation with God's desire and intention for our good health.

Helpful Prayer Patterns

Motivated by our desire to be obedient to Christ and out of our compassion for others we can pray from the heart as the Holy Spirit directs us. However, those who serve on prayer teams sometimes ask for guidelines. The following examples are not to be taken as the only way to pray with others, but rather to provide helpful prayer patterns.

• Lord Jesus Christ, strengthen and heal (name of person). May your healing love and healing power flow into his/her life. Banish all pain and sickness and sin. Give him/her the blessings of health in body, mind, spirit, and relationships.

We thank you and ask these things in your Holy Name. Amen.

- These hands are laid upon you in the Name of the Father, the Son, and the Holy Spirit. May the power of God's indwelling presence heal you of all illnesses of body, mind, and spirit, so that you may serve God with a loving heart and a willing spirit. Amen.

- Thank you, Lord Jesus, for this time of Holy Communion with you and with each other. We now lift into your light and love (name of person). Touch him/her with your healing power. Bring him/her wholeness and new life in body, mind, spirit, and relationships. For doing all this we thank you and give you the glory. Amen.

Praying with others calls for sensitivity to each person's situation, emotional state, and spiritual openness. Constantly seek the Holy Spirit's guidance and wisdom. Rigid rules do not exist in this ministry. Be flexible. Keep these guidelines (adapted from Wagner, *An Adventure in Healing and Wholeness*, 139) in mind. We can pray:

- with or without the laying on of hands,
- with or without anointing oil,
- with formal or informal prayers,
- with or without accompanying music,
- with silent or spoken prayers,
- with the body posture that is most comfortable for all in the prayer circle.

Suggestions When Serving on a Prayer Team

1. Before the worship service begins, the prayer team members have a word of prayer with each other and discuss their pattern of praying with others.
2. In more formal healing services, especially if there are several prayer teams, the pastor or another worship leader may invite the prayer teams to come forward for a commissioning prayer, inviting the Holy Spirit to bless and anoint each one on behalf of the gathered congregation.

3. Memorize and practice this team pattern called L–A–P (adapted from Wagner, *An Adventure in Healing and Wholeness*, 139–40):

Listen (L): Listen to the prayer request. Ask each one who comes to your prayer station:
Do you have a special prayer concern today?
—Or—
What would you like for us to pray about right now?

Anoint (A): Anoint the forehead with oil making the sign of the cross. You may use a thumb or forefinger. The traditional anointing pattern is to pray to God, the Father, through the Son, in the Holy Spirit. Others may feel more inclined to pray by simply addressing Jesus. Then each one on the team gently touches the one who came forward with the laying on of hands. Sample invocations:
"I anoint you in the Name of God: Father, Son, and Holy Spirit, let us pray . . ."
"I anoint you in the Name of Jesus, let us pray . . ."

Pray (P): Pray with the person who has been anointed with oil. The prayer partner who listened to the prayer request offers a brief, audible prayer. Everyone on the team is in an attitude of focused faith, compassion, and prayer.

Additional Considerations When Praying with Others

- Be brief in public prayer ministry. It is not necessary to have lengthy prayers or to rehearse the details of the problem to God who already knows.
- Confidentiality is a must. Keep all revealed personal issues and problems at the altar or prayer station.
- Those who come for prayer with complicated personal issues may be open to counseling and continuing prayer

ministry after the healing service ends. Offer a brief prayer and then suggest that the person remain at the close of the service for further ministry or to make an appointment with the pastor to return at another time. This is a courtesy to the congregation and gives a helpful option to those who desire additional help.

• Team members who want personal prayers for healing and wholeness will pray with one another after ministering to the congregation (adapted from Wagner, *An Adventure in Healing and Wholeness*, 140).

Our goal is to concentrate on the presence of the healing Christ, to focus on the problem solver, rather than on the problem. We want to be more intentional in using spiritual therapy in the healing process. "As Archbishop Richard C. Trent said, 'We must not conceive prayer as an overcoming of God's reluctance, but a laying hold of [God's] highest willingness'" (James K. Wagner, *Blessed to be a Blessing*, [Nashville: Upper Room Books, 1980], 58).

MODELS FOR HEALING SERVICES

(This material is adapted from Wagner, An Adventure in Healing and Wholeness, 136–38, where these models were originally presented as "methods.")

In-the-Pew Model

Everyone stays in the pews. Prayer concerns and joys may be informally voiced by the congregation or written on prayer request cards for the ushers to gather and take to the pastor. These can be incorporated into the pastoral prayer and may or may not name specific persons and situations. Some pastors invite the congregation to form small groups in the pews for simultaneous personal prayer ministry as part of the Sunday morning service.

Silent Model

Persons requesting prayer are invited to come forward to the communion railing, altar, or chancel area. They may kneel, stand, or sit. Individually they receive the ministry of laying on of hands with a brief, silent prayer. Anointing oil is optional. The person laying on of hands may be a clergyperson or a layperson. The only word spoken is *Amen* at the conclusion of the silent prayer.

United Model

Persons requesting prayer are invited to come forward to the communion railing, altar, or chancel area. They may kneel or stand. The minister prays with two persons at a time, placing a hand on each head. Individual prayer concerns are not expressed. The minister offers a brief, spoken prayer, similar to a blessing. Anointing oil is optional.

Team Model

Two or three persons serve on a prayer team. Those requesting prayer are invited to come forward to the communion railing or other designated prayer stations. Each one who comes forward has an opportunity to voice his or her specific concern or request to the prayer team. All on the team lay on hands and join in silent or spoken prayer. Anointing oil is usually administered.

Holy Communion and Healing Services

This is sometimes called "The Sacramental Model." Each of the four models listed above may be incorporated into a Holy Communion liturgy. Prayers for healing and wholeness may be offered before or after the distribution of the bread and cup.

Other Models Practiced in Churches Today

• On Holy Communion Sundays, persons desiring the ministry of prayer with laying on of hands and anointing oil are invited to come with the last group to the Lord's Table.

- On Holy Communion Sundays, all who come to the Lord's Table are offered the ministry of healing prayer after receiving the bread and the cup. Following a table dismissal prayer, those who remain receive personal prayer with laying on of hands and anointing oil.
- In every worship service, persons desiring the ministry of healing prayer are requested to come forward after the benediction. Others are dismissed and leave the sanctuary. Lay prayer teams may be assigned in advance to be ready to offer prayer ministry with laying on of hands and anointing oil.
- Incorporated into the pastoral prayer on Sunday mornings is a special prayer time at the altar for those who wish to come forward. As the music plays quietly in the background, the pastor and designated laypersons may pray individually with each one. Some may come for silent, personal prayer.
- Some churches offer opportunities for healing prayer in connection with another worship service or scheduled activity in the church:
  — before Sunday school and Sunday worship services,
  — between Sunday morning services,
  — around noon on Sundays after the other services end,
  — before or after midweek Bible study,
  — Saturday or Sunday evening services,
  — noontime services during the week,
  — early on weekday mornings.

Consult denominational worship books for additional models of healing services.

A BASIC PATTERN

Gathering and Centering

Silence is always appropriate when coming together for worship. If music is played, let it be quiet, meditative, and relaxing.

Welcome and Greeting

Announcements, introductions, and any instructions for the healing service are offered here.

Hymn of Praise

This could also be a medley of praise songs.

Opening Prayer

This prayer can be printed and prayed in unison or offered by the worship leader.

Holy Scripture Readings

Focus on a psalm or a healing story from the Gospels. See the list of "Biblical Healing Passages" at the back of this book.

Message of Healing and Hope

Alternatives to a brief homily could be silent reflection and meditation on the previously read scripture or someone could give a personal testimony to God's healing.

Response to the Word

This may include one or more of the following: affirmation of faith, pastoral prayer, invitation to receive the abundant life in Christ, special music, or an offering.

Prayers for Others

Intercessory prayers are offered for those with special needs who are not present in the healing service.

Confession of Sin and Assurance of Pardon

The Peace of Christ

Offer one another signs of reconciliation and love.

Hymn of Preparation

Sacrament of Holy Communion (Optional)

When Holy Communion is celebrated, it is recommended that prayer teams take the Communion elements first and then station themselves to pray with those desiring prayer ministry during and after the distribution of the bread and cup.

Prayers for Personal Healing of Body, Mind, Spirit, and Relationships

Following the instructions in James 5:14-16, anointing oil and laying on of hands with prayer are offered to the congregation. Persons may come forward for their personal needs or on behalf of another. Recommend quiet music in the background.

Sharing Our Joys and Thanksgivings

This concludes the healing service on a positive note by inviting the gathered body of Christ to share briefly answers to prayers or something good happening in their lives. This informal sharing reinforces the blessings and benefits of an intentional healing ministry.

Closing Prayer

Hymn of Praise or Dedication

Dismissal with Blessing

EXAMPLES OF HEALING SERVICES

The guidelines in this chapter have been provided for you to use in developing a healing service ministry in your church. Consider now the twelve healing services that follow in chapters 3 through 14, which have been designed and tested in a variety of settings and situations.

CHAPTER THREE

A CONTEMPORARY WORSHIP SERVICE

This healing service is designed for a contemporary worship style:

- Worship leaders dress informally;
- Order of Worship is uncomplicated, easy to follow;
- Words to the songs, scripture readings, congregational prayers/ responses, and announcements are projected on a screen;
- The sermon/message is presented in a teaching/conversational manner;
- Holy Communion is optional;
- Music accompaniment is provided by keyboard, guitars, drums, and other instruments;
- Praise/prayer songs and choruses are carefully chosen and rehearsed to enhance the worship experience.

Gathering for Praise and Worship
(Praise music can be played and/or sung.)

Words of Welcome

Announcements

Opening Medley of Praise Songs

Invite the Congregation to Greet One Another

Centering Prayer Song

Opening Prayer

Great and Merciful God, as we gather to praise and worship you, we come today knowing that even though you love us as we are, you love us too much to let us stay the way we are. Open our minds, soften our hearts, unite our spirits, and make us more receptive to all that you desire for each of us. This we pray in the name of your Son Jesus, our Savior and Healer. Amen.

Holy Scripture Reading

(Choose a passage from the healing ministry of Jesus)

- John 4:46-53
- Mark 8:22-26

Message

(Because the healing ministry may be unfamiliar to some, this is valuable teaching time. The homilist can inform, teach, and share some ways to respond to God's desire for our health and wholeness in body, mind, spirit, and relationships.)

Praying for Others (Intercessory Prayer)

I invite you to select from your personal prayer lists, someone not present in this worship service, one person whom you bring in your hearts to be blessed and helped by God.

(Pause for silent reflection.)

Now turn to someone sitting near you and share that name and situation. Please be brief.

(Pause)

Now let us pray silently for the names given to us.

(Pause)

Gracious and loving God,
what a special privilege it is to name in prayer

20

those precious persons that you have created
and placed on our hearts and minds today.
We bring each one to you in the light and love of Jesus,
thanking you for helping and healing. Amen.

Offering
(Receive this in response to God's limitless grace and blessings.)

Special Music
(Build on the worship theme and move the congregation to the time of healing prayers.)

Prayers for Healing of Body, Mind, Spirit, and Relationships

Hear these instructions in the letter of James 5:14-16:

> Are any among you sick? They should call for the elders of the church and have them pray over them, anointing them with oil in the name of the Lord. The prayer of faith will save the sick, and the Lord will raise them up; and anyone who has committed sins will be forgiven. Therefore confess your sins to one another, and pray for one another, so that you may be healed.

Prayer of Confession

Almighty and most merciful God,
  you know the thoughts of our hearts.
We confess that we have sinned against you
  and done evil in your sight.
We have transgressed your holy laws.
We have disregarded your Word and Sacrament.
Forgive us, O Lord.
Give us grace and power to put away all hurtful things,
  that, being delivered from the bondage of sin,
    we may bring forth fruit worthy of repentance,
and from this moment may ever walk in your holy ways;
  through Jesus Christ our Lord. Amen.
(All offer prayers of confession in silence.)

Assurance of Pardon

If we confess our sins, [God] who is faithful and just will forgive us our sins and cleanse us from all unrighteousness (1 John 1:9).

The almighty and merciful Lord, grant . . . remission of all our sins, true repentance, amendment of life, and the grace and consolation of [the] Holy Spirit. Amen (*The Book of Common Prayer*, 1928, 24).

Invitation for Healing Prayers

Following the instructions in the letter of James, you are invited to come forward for healing prayers with anointing oil. You may come for yourself or on behalf of another person. If you are unable to come forward, tell an usher; a prayer team will come to you. (*Instrumental music, played softly, and quiet singing are appropriate.*)

Prayer of Thanksgiving

(*After the prayers for healing*)
Surely your presence, O Lord, is in this place.
We bow with gratitude to you for all
the ways you are blessing us now
and will continue to bless us in the days ahead.
In the name above all names,
in the Name of Jesus we thank you. Amen.

Praise Song

Dismissal with Blessing

And now may the words that we have said and sung,
let us believe in our hearts;
and what we believe in our hearts,
may we live in our lives, for the glory of God
this day and evermore. Amen!

CHAPTER FOUR

HEALING SERVICE FOR SMALL GROUP SETTINGS

This brief service (twenty-five to thirty minutes) could be offered before or after other scheduled meetings. Notice the absence of hymn singing, homily, special music, and offering; although these and other worshipful acts can be included. After serving the bread and the cup, the presiding minister might say: "Those who desire personal prayers for healing and wholeness may remain where you are; others arise and go in the peace of Christ." The prayer team would then anoint and pray with each one who stays.

Gathering Music

Greetings and Welcome in the Name of the Risen Christ

Opening Prayer

Creator, Redeemer, Sustainer God,
grant that we may have
    the peace of Christ in our hearts,

the wisdom of Christ in our work,
and the love of Christ in our lives,
so that we may be a blessing to others
and bring honor to your Holy Name. Amen.

Act of Praise
(A reading from the Psalms would be appropriate, perhaps Psalm 103:1-18.)

Silent Reflection

Prayers for Others
It has been said that intercessory prayer is love on its knees. Let all of us be in an attitude of loving concern and thanksgiving as prayer requests are shared *(invite informal sharing from the congregation)*.

Prayer

O God, you are the only source of health and healing, the Spirit of calm and the central peace of this universe. Make these for whom we now pray very conscious of your healing nearness. Touch their eyes that they may see you; open their ears that they may hear your voice; enter their hearts that they may know your love. Overshadow their souls and bodies with your presence, that they may partake of your strength, your love, your abundant life. In Jesus' name we pray. Amen.

Holy Scripture Reading
(Choose a passage from the healing ministry of Jesus.)
- Mark 10:46-52
- Matthew 20:29-34.

Reflection on God's Word
(This can be a brief commentary or moments of silence.)

Confession of Our Sins

Lord Jesus Christ, you are the way of peace.
Come into the brokenness of our lives and our land
    with your healing love.
Help us to be willing to bow before you
    in true repentance,
    and to bow to one another in real forgiveness.
By the fire of your Holy Spirit,
    melt our hard hearts and consume
    the pride and prejudice that may separate us.
Fill us, O Christ, with your perfect love,
    which casts out our fear
and bind us together in that unity
    which you share with the Father and the Holy Spirit.
Amen.

Silent Confession

Assurance of Pardon

Hear the Good News.
Christ himself is the means by which our sins are forgiven.
In the name of Jesus Christ you are forgiven!
In the name of Jesus Christ you are forgiven!
Thanks be to God. Amen!

The Peace

Let us offer one another signs of peace and love in Christ.

The Sacrament of Holy Communion

Words of Institution for the Lord's Supper
Great Thanksgiving Prayer
The Lord's Prayer
Invitation: all are invited to the Lord's Table.
(If needed, give a word of instruction.)

Prayers for the Healing of the Body, Mind, Spirit, and Relationships

You are also invited to come forward for personal prayer for yourself or on behalf of another person. You may express your prayer concern to the prayer team, who will anoint you with oil, making the sign of the cross on your forehead and will gently lay on hands with prayer. Let us be in prayer for one another.

Sharing of Thanksgivings and Joys

Dismissal with Blessing (Romans 15:13)

May the God of hope fill you with all joy
    and peace in believing,
so that you may abound in hope
    by the power of the Holy Spirit.

CHAPTER FIVE

A QUIET, MEDITATIVE SERVICE

This healing service can be used with large or small gatherings of worshipers. The duration of the service is determined by the length of the homily and the number of persons who come forward for healing prayers. A helpful guideline is to have one prayer team for every twelve to fifteen persons in attendance. Holy Communion is not listed in the Order of Service, but could be celebrated.

Gathering in Silence for Prayer and Meditation

Greetings and Welcome in the Name of Christ

As we come seeking God's healing, wholeness, and salvation, we come in faith recalling the instructions of the Apostle James:

> Are any among you sick? They should call for the elders of the church and have them pray over them, anointing them with oil in the name of the Lord. The prayer of faith will save the sick, and the Lord will raise them up; and anyone who has committed sins will be forgiven. Therefore, confess your sins to one another and pray for one another, so that you may be

healed. The prayer of the righteous is powerful and effective. (James 5:14-16)

Opening Prayer

Creator and Healer of the world,
  help us see our part in your work
  of healing our world and its wounded people.
Show us what needs to be torn down
  and what needs to be built up,
  that all people may live in peace and safety,
  enjoying fullness of life. **Amen.**

(From Number 397, *Upper Room Worshipbook*, copyright © 2006 by Mary Lou Redding. Used by permission of Upper Room Books®, www.bookstore.upperroom.org, 1-800-972-0433)

Hymn

- "Sanctuary," by John Thompson and Randy Scruggs
- "Father, I Adore You," by Terrye Coelho

Confession of Our Sins

Compassionate and understanding God, we come to you asking for another chance to become the kind of people you created us to be. We acknowledge before you and one another that we have been less than honest in confessing our sins, especially the ones we try to hide from you and even from ourselves. Stir up within us a genuine desire to pray as the psalmist prayed:

Who can detect their errors?
  Clear me from hidden faults.
. . . .
Let the words of my mouth and the meditation of my heart
  be acceptable to you,
  O LORD, my rock and my redeemer. (Psalm 19:12, 14)

Silent Confession

Assurance of Pardon

Hear and receive the Good News.
In the name of Jesus Christ you are forgiven!
In the name of Jesus Christ you are forgiven!
Praise be to God!
Praise be to God! Amen!

Passing the Peace

As God's forgiven and accepted people, share with one another signs of reconciliation and love.

Holy Scripture Reading

(Choose a passage from the healing ministry of Jesus.)

- Luke 5:12-16
- Luke 17:11-19

Silent Reflection on the Word or a Message of Hope

Prayers for Healing of Body, Mind, Spirit, and Relationships

You are invited to come forward for prayer on behalf of another person or for yourself. We will anoint and pray with you following the instructions of James 5:14-16.

Sharing our Joys and Thanksgivings

Closing Prayer

It has been good, Gracious and Loving God,
    to be here today with you and with
    the gathered body of Christ.
Accept our heartfelt gratitude and thanksgiving,
    as we give you the glory, honor, and praise. Amen!

Hymn
- "Precious Name," by Lydia Baxter
- "God Be With You," by Jeremiah E. Rankin

Dismissal with Blessing (Ephesians 3:20)
Now to [God] who by the power at work within us is able to accomplish
abundantly far more than all we can ask or imagine,
to [God] be glory in the church and in Christ Jesus to all generations,
forever and ever. Amen.

HEALING SERVICE FOR A CHAPEL SETTING

This reflective, meditative healing service works well in a chapel or outdoor setting. The open ending allows the participants to remain as long as they wish for time alone with God.

Gathering Music

Greetings and Welcome in the Name of the Risen Christ

(This is a time for announcements, introductions, and instructions related to the healing service.)

Opening Prayer

Loving Lord Jesus, before your trials of suffering
    you prayed that all your disciples might be one in Spirit.
Grant that we may be bound together in love
    for one another and in obedience to you,
    so that the world may see and believe. Amen.

Act of Praise

(Choose a reading from the Psalms, such as Psalm 63:1-8.)

Moments of Reflection

In silence let us reflect on God's Word in Psalm 63, as we receive the healing touch of the Holy Spirit in our hearts, minds, and spirits.

Prayers for Others

Bear one another's burdens, and in this way
   you will fulfill the law of Christ (Galatians 6:2).
Let us share the special needs
of those who are on our hearts and minds today.
(After voicing the community's prayer requests for others, pray the corporate prayer of intercession.)

Our healing and saving Christ,
   we place each of these precious ones
   into your hands, the Great Physician.
May our faith and trust in you assist in their recovery.
Help each of them and each of us
   in our personal situations.
Give us, we pray, your hope for the future
   and the joyful experience of your presence
   in our lives today. Amen.

Holy Scripture Reading

(Choose a passage from the healing ministry of Jesus.)
   • Matthew 8:14-15
   • Mark 7:31-37.

Reflection on God's Word

(Offer a brief commentary or invite the congregation to share a few moments of silence.)

Call to Confession

Let us test and examine our ways, and return to the Lord! If we say we have no sin, we deceive ourselves, and the truth is not in us. If we confess our sins, God is faithful and just, and will forgive our sins and cleanse us from all wrongdoing. In this confidence let us confess before God and one another.

Prayer of Confession

Creator God, you have placed a treasure
 deep inside each of us—
a moment of insight, a mountain of affirmation,
 a sense of your love.
Yet how often we treat one another with a harshness
 that bruises the soul or an indifference
 that wounds the spirit.
We have been given the precious gift
 of caring for each other,
 guarding each other's light
 and proclaiming the gospel of love.
Forgive us for handling this gift
 with heavy hands and hardened hearts.
Open our eyes to the wonder of each person
 and to your abundant grace
that heals our brokenness and restores our faith. Amen.

Silent Confession

Assurance of Pardon

Hear the Good News.
Christ himself is the means by which our sins are forgiven.
In the name of Jesus Christ you are forgiven!
In the Name of Jesus Christ you are forgiven!
Thanks be to God! Amen!

The Peace

Let us offer one another signs of peace and love in Christ.

The Sacrament of Holy Communion and Prayers for Healing

Words of Institution for the Lord's Supper

The Great Thanksgiving Prayer

The Lord's Prayer (unison)

Invitation

All are invited to come to the Lord's Table. After receiving the Bread and the Cup you may return to your seats or remain for personal prayer for yourself or on behalf of another person. You may express your concern to the prayer team who will anoint you with oil, make the sign of the cross on your forehead, and lay on hands with prayer (see James 5:14-16).

Sharing of Personal Blessings and Joys

Prayer of Thanksgiving

Now thank we all our God, with hearts and hands and voices,
who wondrous things has done, in whom this world rejoices;
who from our mothers' arms has blessed us on our way
with countless gifts of love, and still is ours today. Amen.

("Now Thank We All Our God," stanza 1, by Martin Rinkart, trans. by Catherine Winkworth)

Time Alone with God

You are most welcome to stay as long as you like for personal prayer and time alone with God. Continue to relax in God's presence and experience God's peace that surpasses all human understanding and guards our hearts and minds in Christ. Amen.

CHAPTER SEVEN

A TRADITIONAL HOLY COMMUNION SERVICE

Holy Communion and healing go together. "Martin Luther, the sixteenth-century reformer, called the Eucharist [Holy Communion] 'the medicine of God' because he knew people who received healing at the Lord's table . . . Morton Kelsey, an Episcopal priest, calls [Holy Communion] a healing sacrament because we receive love (the love of Christ) and then we share this love with others, and that is healing" (Wagner, *An Adventure in Healing and Wholeness*, 94).

This traditional service of Holy Communion can be expanded to include additional elements of worship. The Prayer of Great Thanksgiving is purposely not printed. Consult other worship resources for Great Thanksgivings designed around the Christian year or for special emphases.

Gathering Music

Greetings and Welcome to the Body of Christ

Call to Worship (Proverbs 3:5-8)
Trust in the LORD with all your heart,
and do not rely on your own insight.

In all your ways acknowledge [the LORD],
  [who] will make straight your paths.
Do not be wise in your own eyes;
  fear the LORD, and turn away from evil.
It will be a healing for your flesh
  and a refreshment for your body.

Opening Prayer

Almighty and everlasting God,
creator of our body, mind, and spirit,
we call upon your love and your mercy
so that we may be healed, restored, and renewed
to serve you; through Jesus Christ our Lord. Amen.

Hymn or Medley of Praise Songs

- "Great Is Thy Faithfulness," by Thomas O. Chisholm
- "God Will Take Care of You," by Civilla D. Martin
- "He Is Lord," by Anonymous (based on Philippians 2:9-11)

Holy Scripture Reading

- John 5:1-9, 14-15

A Message of Healing and Hope: "Do You Want to Be Healed?"

Let us revisit that scene by the pool of Bethesda in the city of Jerusalem. One day into this sea of homeless street people came Jesus and his disciples. For some reason unknown to us, Jesus selected one man who had been paralyzed for thirty-eight years. Perhaps Jesus had met this man on other visits to Jerusalem. Perhaps Jesus knew something about this man, who is not named in the story.

The first words from Jesus to this man who could not walk are very significant words for us, especially when we have been sick or incapacitated for a long time. To paraphrase the question:

"Tell me, do you want to be healed?"

"Do you really want to get better?"

"Do you truly desire to be able to walk again?"

That may, at first, seem like a "no-brainer." Why wouldn't this man want to walk again?

Yet, change is tough, even for the right reasons. Consider these penetrating questions:

"What are some of the benefits of your illness?"

"What personal privileges would you lose if you got better?"

Sometimes it's more comfortable to stay unhealthy than to put yourself through the necessary, therapeutic steps to restored health.

Some people say they want to be healed, but actually block the healing process: sickness becomes a lifestyle. They go to doctors, yet seem to enjoy poor health.

Some refuse to take the recommended therapy or medicine. When an illness is diagnosed as incurable, some people give up the will to live and do not explore spiritual help and alternative therapies. The word "incurable" is not in the Bible.

Some people may want to get well, but are convinced that the cure that helps others will not work for them.

The paralyzed man in the story had convinced himself that he would never get any better because the only cure he knew was to be the first to get into the Pool of Bethesda when an angel disturbed the water. As he said to Jesus, "Sir, I have no one to put me into the pool when the water is stirred up; and while I am making my way, someone else steps down ahead of me" (John 5:7).

Notice carefully how Jesus helped and healed this despondent, discouraged man, who had, no doubt, given up all hope of ever walking again. The fact that Jesus was paying attention to him may have instilled a glimmer of hope, a necessary factor in the healing process. Jesus restored this man to wholeness and health at least three ways:

Physical healing: He did get up and walk.

Mental healing: Jesus helped him overcome his negative attitude and deal with the hard question: "Do you want to be healed?"

Spiritual healing: Later that day Jesus and the man met in the temple where Jesus assured him that his sins were forgiven and he had a restored relationship with God.

Although this story does not mention healing the man's relationships with the other street people, he had to be bitter, resentful, and angry. All of these negative emotions can block one's healing and become barriers in relating to God and to people in healthy ways.

It is quite believable that Jesus also assisted this man in coping and working through his fractured relationships with the therapy of forgiveness. This is only a guess, but not beyond a possibility.

This amazing story in John's Gospel gives each of us hope and portrays Jesus as the holistic Savior. Because Jesus loves the whole person, his goal was and is to help each person become whole and healthy in every area of life.

Closing question: Is there an area of your life that has been less than whole and healthy for a long time, or even for a short time? If so, how would you answer Jesus if he asked you the same question he asked the man in the story: "Tell me. Do you really want to get well?"

Response to the Word
(This may include a song, a psalm, an affirmation of faith, and/or acts of renewal and commitment.)

- Psalm 145:8-21 as a responsive reading. (See *The United Methodist Hymnal*, 857-58 for an example.)

Prayers for Others
(This can be a litany of intercessions and/or concerns from the congregation. Invite the congregation to share informally the names of persons for whom they are praying. These names could also be written on cards, given to the ushers, and placed on the altar. After some moments for silent prayers, this intercessory prayer for healing could be prayed in unison by the congregation or offered by the liturgist.)

O God,

Here is my sister – overwhelmed with grief and pain,
    tearfully seeking your healing love.
Here is my brother – anxious, lonely, and frightened,
    uncertain even how to pray.

Do not pass them by, Lord Jesus!
Send the light of your redeeming grace upon them.
Welcome them back into the arms of your loving embrace.
Comfort them in their grief and heal their infirmities;
Lead them in your way of Love,
    by the power of the Holy Spirit we pray. Amen.

(From Number 31, *Upper Room Worshipbook*, copyright © 2006
by Jerry Haas. Used by permission of Upper Room Books®,
www.bookstore.upperroom.org, 1-800-972-0433)

Invitation

Christ our Lord invites to his table all who love him, who
earnestly repent of their sin and who seek to live in peace with
one another. Therefore, let us confess our sin before God and
before one another.

Confession and Pardon

Merciful God, we admit that too often we try to cover up our sin-
fulness with pleasant-sounding words, generous deeds, and helpful activities. We need your help. Forgive us when we bypass your
desires. Forgive us when we lose sight of your values and yearn-
ings for each of us. Guide us in getting our priorities straight. As
Psalm 51:17 reminds us so powerfully:
    The sacrifice acceptable to God is a broken spirit;
        a broken and contrite heart, O God, you will not despise.

(*All offer prayers of confession in silence.*)
    The LORD is gracious and merciful,
        slow to anger and abounding in steadfast love (Psalm 145:8).
    The almighty and merciful Lord, grant [us] . . . remission of all
        our sins,
        true repentance, amendment of life,
        and the grace and consolation of [the] Holy Spirit. Amen.

(*The Book of Common Prayer*, 1928, 24)

39

The Peace

Let us offer one another signs of love and peace.

Offering

As forgiven and reconciled people, we offer ourselves and our gifts to God.

Communion Hymn

- "Jesu, Jesu," by Tom Colvin
- "Jesus, We Are Here," by Patrick Matsikenyiri

Sacrament of Holy Communion

The Prayer of Great Thanksgiving

The Lord's Prayer (unison)

Prayer of Thanksgiving over the Oil

O God, the giver of health and salvation,
 we give thanks to you for the gift of oil.
As your holy apostles anointed many who were sick and
 healed them,
 so pour your Holy Spirit on us and on this gift,
 that those who in faith and repentance receive this anointing
 may be made whole;
through Jesus Christ our Lord. Amen.

(*The Book of Common Prayer*, 1979, alt. as published in *The United Methodist Book of Worship*, 620)

The Invitation to Communion

The Lord's Table is open to all.

Prayers for Healing of the Body, Mind, Spirit, and Relationships

You are also invited to come forward for personal prayer for yourself or on behalf of another person. You may express your concern to the prayer team who will anoint you with oil, make the sign of the cross on your forehead, and gently lay on hands with prayer. Let us all be in prayer for one another.

Sharing Our Thanksgivings and Joys

Closing Prayer

Eternal God, we give you thanks for this holy mystery
   in which you have given yourself to us.
Grant that we may go into the world
   in the strength of your Spirit,
to give ourselves for others,
in the name of Jesus Christ our Lord. Amen.

(From A *Service of Word and Table I,* copyright 1972, 1980, 1985, 1989, The United Methodist Publishing House, as published in *The United Methodist Hymnal,* 11)

Hymn

- "I Want to Walk as a Child of the Light," by Kathleen Thomerson
- "Pass It On," by Kurt Kaiser

Benediction and Sending Forth

Go forth in peace.
The grace of the Lord Jesus Christ, the love of God,
   and the communion of the Holy Spirit
   be with you all. Amen.

(From A *Service of Word and Table I,* copyright 1972, 1980, 1985, 1989, The United Methodist Publishing House, as published in *The United Methodist Hymnal,* 11)

CHAPTER EIGHT

A COMMUNION SERVICE OF BIBLICAL HEALING STORIES

This Holy Communion-based healing service could be offered at the regular Sunday morning worship hour. The Prayer of Great Thanksgiving focuses on several healing stories in the Bible. Anthems and other special music, scripture lessons, and an offering can be inserted in appropriate places.

Greetings and Welcome in the Name of the Risen Christ

As we come seeking God's healing, wholeness, and salvation, we come in faith recalling the instructions of the Apostle James, who wrote:

> Are any among you suffering? They should pray. Are any cheerful? They should sing songs of praise. Are any among you sick? They should call for the elders of the church and have them pray over them, anointing them with oil in the name of the Lord. The prayer of faith will save the sick, and the Lord will raise them up; and anyone who has committed sins will be forgiven. Therefore, confess your sins to one another and pray

for one another, so that you may be healed. The prayer of the righteous is powerful and effective. (James 5:13-16)

Call to Worship

Praise be to God, in whose presence there is peace and harmony.
**Praise be to God, in whose presence there is love,
forgiveness, and acceptance.**
Praise be to God, in whose presence there is healing,
wholeness, and salvation.
Praise be to God!

Hymn of Praise

- "All Hail the Power of Jesus' Name," by Edward Perronet, alt. by John Rippon
- "What a Friend We Have in Jesus," by Joseph M. Scriven

Opening Prayer

God of mercy and tenderness, we need your healing touch today. Heal us of all sicknesses of body, mind, spirit, and relationships; heal us of those illnesses that prevent us from becoming the people you want us to become. Remove from our lives the barriers that hinder our progress. We admit, gracious God, that we often are afraid. We fear the unknown. We fear change. We fear pain. We fear sickness. Release us from the fears that paralyze us. Reach down deep inside us, and gently heal those painful wounds that cause us so much distress. Heal those memories and scars that confuse our thinking and distort our personalities. We worship you and pray in the name and the power of Jesus Christ our Lord. Amen.

Holy Scripture Reading

(Choose a passage from the healing ministry of Jesus.)

- Luke 7:1-10

Sermon and/or Testimony to Healing

(Personal stories that witness to the continuing healing ministry of Christ in our lives, in our church, and in our community communicate

powerful messages. Prior to the healing service the pastor could contact someone who has a personal healing story to share. This could be integrated in the sermon, stand alone, or presented in an interview format, with the pastor asking leading questions.)

Prayers for Others

Let each of us be in an attitude of loving concern as prayer requests are expressed. To each request the congregation may respond:

Thank you, Lord, for helping and healing.

(Following the prayer requests, the worship leader may offer this prayer.)

Blessed and Compassionate Jesus,
   we bring for your loving care and protection,
on the stretchers of our prayers,
   all those who are sick in mind, body, or soul.
Take from them all fears
   and help them put their trust in you.
Cleanse them of all resentment, jealousy, self-pity, pride,
   or anything else that might block your healing power.
Fill them with the sense of your loving presence,
   that they may experience
   your kingdom of love in their hearts.
Touch them with your divine, transforming mercy,
   that they may be healed and live to glorify you,
   this day and forevermore.
In thankfulness we pray. Amen.

Confession

Let us pray together:
God of all compassion and tenderness,
we humbly confess our impatience
   when our lives do not work out in the manner
   we ourselves have prescribed.
We confess that we tend to demand
   instant results from you.

In so doing, we miss the miracles of your
   step-by-step process of healing and wholeness.
Forgive our lack of trust in your mercy.
Help us recognize the healing ministry
   of your Holy Spirit as we encounter you
   in every area of our daily lives,
   even in this moment of worship.
In the name and compassion of your son, Jesus Christ,
   forgive and renew each of us. Amen.
(Pause for silent confession.)

The Assurance of Pardon

Hear the good news:
Christ died for us while we were yet sinners;
   that proves God's love toward us.
In the name of Jesus Christ you are forgiven.
In the name of Jesus Christ you are forgiven.
Glory to God! Amen!

The Peace

Let us offer one another signs of reconciliation and love as we
pass the peace of Christ among us.

Communion Hymn

- "Holy Ground," by Geron Davis
- "Spirit Song," by John Wimber

The Great Thanksgiving

The Lord be with you.
And also with you.
Lift up your hearts.
We lift them up to the Lord.
Let us give thanks to the Lord our God.
It is right to give our thanks and praise.
Gracious God, you have shown us your healing power down
through the ages. When Jacob was afraid as he went out to meet

Esau, you brought reconciliation between the two brothers. When an evil spirit came upon Saul, you sent young David to play music on his lute so that Saul was refreshed. When a plague was ravishing the nation, King David confessed his sin of pride and prayed before you so that the plague was lifted. When Naaman, the commander of the army of Syria, sought healing from leprosy, the prophet Elisha sent him to wash in the Jordan River and Naaman was healed by the power of God.

When Simon Peter's mother-in-law was sick with a fever, Jesus touched her hand and she rose and served them. When a leper knelt before Jesus and said, "Lord, if you will, you can make me clean." Jesus reached out his hand and touched him and said, "I will; be clean." When a woman who had a flow of blood for twelve years touched the fringe of Jesus' garment, power went forth and she was healed. When a man lame from birth begged for money from Peter and John, the disciples offered him the gift of healing, and his feet and ankles were made strong at the gate outside the Jerusalem Temple. Because of these and all your compassionate acts of healing and the glory of your salvation, we join with the saints on earth and the saints above in the song of unending praise:

Holy, holy, holy Lord, God of power and might,
Heaven and earth are full of your glory.
Hosanna in the highest.
Blessed is he who comes in the name of the Lord.
Hosanna in the highest.

Holy are you and blessed is your son Jesus Christ, who lived among us and who knew human pain and suffering. He healed the sick, fed the hungry, and ate with sinners. He cast out demons and showed many people the way to you through faith. On the night in which he gave himself up for us, he took bread, gave thanks to you, broke the bread, and offered it to the disciples who were gathered within the room. Jesus said, "Take this and eat; this is my body broken for you. Do this in remembrance of me." After supper, Jesus took a cup of wine. Again he gave thanks to you, shared the cup with the disciples, and said, "This is the cup of the new covenant poured out for you and for many for the forgiveness of sins. Drink from this, all of you." Then they went to a garden where Jesus prayed. After he was betrayed, Jesus was arrested and brought to trial and then he died on a cross. When the powers of death had done their worst, Jesus was raised from the dead so that at the name of Jesus every knee may bow and every tongue confess that Jesus Christ is Lord. We celebrate this great victory and pray that we may now be a living sacrifice, holy and pleasing to you, so that our lives may proclaim the mystery of faith:

Christ has died.
Christ is risen.
Christ will come again.

God of love, pour out your Holy Spirit upon us so that those who suffer from sickness in body, mind, spirit, or relationships may be restored and made whole. By the power of your Holy Spirit may these gifts of bread and wine become for us the Body and Blood of our Savior Jesus Christ. Make us instruments of your peace for the healing of the world and the reconciliation of the nations. Through your son Jesus Christ with the Holy Spirit in your holy church, all glory and honor are yours, Almighty God, now and forever. Amen.

And now with the confidence of the children of God, let us pray the Lord's Prayer. "**Our Father . . .**"

The Invitation

The Lord's Table is open to all.

Giving and Receiving the Bread and the Cup

Prayer of Thanksgiving over the Oil

O God, the giver of health and salvation,
  we give thanks to you for the gift of oil.
As your holy apostles anointed many who were sick and
      healed them,
    so pour your Holy Spirit on us and on this gift,
  that those who in faith and repentance receive this anointing may be made whole;
through Jesus Christ our Lord. **Amen.**

(*The Book of Common Prayer*, 1979, alt. as published in *The United Methodist Book of Worship*, 620)

Prayers for Healing and Wholeness

You may to come forward for personal prayers for yourself or on behalf of another person. You may express your concern to the prayer team who will anoint you with oil, make the sign of the cross on your forehead, and gently lay on hands with prayer. Let us be in prayer for one another.

Sharing Our Thanksgivings

You are invited to share your joys, thanksgivings, and answers to prayers.

Closing Prayer

God of grace and strength, you are the source of our life and health. In your presence we find help, hope, and wholeness. Send us from this place to be healing reminders of your love to all whose lives we touch. In the Name of Jesus we pray. Amen.

Benediction (Numbers 6:24-26)

The LORD bless you and keep you;
the LORD make his face to shine upon you,
    and be gracious to you;
the LORD lift up his countenance upon you,
    and give you peace. Amen.

Congregational Singing Response

- "Tino tenda Jesu (Thank You, Jesus)," original Shona language translated by Patrick Matsikenyiri
- "Something Beautiful," by Gloria Gaither

Chapter Nine

A Flexible Pattern

Depending on the circumstances, this healing service can be lengthened or abbreviated. The confession and assurance of pardon come early in the order of service. The Doxology and Holy Communion are optional.

Gathering Music

Greetings and Welcome to the Body of Christ

Call to Worship (Psalm 103:1-5, 22)

Bless the LORD, O my soul,
   and all that is within me,
   bless [God's] holy name.
Bless the LORD, O my soul,
   and do not forget all [God's] benefits—
who forgives all your iniquity,
   who heals all your diseases,
who redeems your life from the Pit [of destruction],
   who crowns you with steadfast love and mercy,
who satisfies you with good as long as you live.
   Bless the LORD, O my soul.

Opening Prayer

As we come to worship you and praise your holy name,
    O God,
    remind us of all your blessings undeserved and benefits
        that never quit.
May this moment be for each of us a special time
    for healing and for restoring balance and harmony
        in our lives.
We pray in the Name of Jesus. Amen.

Hymn of Praise

- "Come, Christians, Join to Sing," by Christian Henry Bateman
- "O for a Thousand Tongues to Sing," by Charles Wesley

The Confession (Psalm 51:10-12)

As we quiet ourselves and enter into this special time of confession and openness to God's forgiveness, let us pray verses ten through twelve of Psalm 51 and then offer our silent prayers of confession to God:

Create in me a clean heart, O God,
    and put a new and right spirit within me.
Do not cast me away from your presence,
    and do not take your holy spirit from me.
Restore to me the joy of your salvation,
    and sustain in me a willing spirit.
(All pray prayers of confession silently.)

Assurance of Pardon

In the Name of Jesus Christ, you are forgiven!
In the Name of Jesus Christ, you are forgiven!
Thanks be to God!
Amen and Amen!

Doxology

(Optional, may be said or sung)
Glory be to the Father, and to the Son, and to the Holy Ghost.
As it was in the beginning, is now and ever shall be,
world without end. Amen! Amen!

Holy Scripture Reading

What is the significance of faith in the healing process? Is faith necessary in healing? Does faith heal? Listen closely to these five scripture readings from the healing ministry of Jesus. Try to discover the role that faith played in each story of healing selected from more than two dozen healing stories in the ministry of Jesus. *(Arrange for five different readers to read these healing stories in succession.)*

- Matthew 8:1-4
- Matthew 8:5-13
- Matthew 8:14-15
- Matthew 9:20-22
- Mark 2:1-5, 11-12

Message of Healing and Hope: "Does Faith Heal?"

Research in health care and in ways to stay healthy seems to make the headlines every day. We are learning, for instance, that human beings cannot depend on the medical profession to keep us one hundred percent healthy. Medicine certainly helps; surgical procedures help; psychology helps, but these therapies alone are insufficient for our total health care. Why? Because we are spiritual beings created in the image of God (Genesis 1:26-27).

Ponder this thought: we are not human beings having a spiritual experience; rather, we are spiritual beings having a human experience. Translated that means when we become sick we need to consider our relationship with God and place our faith in God—who not only created us, but also yearns for each of us to be healthy, as evidenced in the healing ministry of Jesus. Medical science is now demonstrating that faith can be a significant factor in the healing process. Increasing numbers of doctors are encouraging their patients to pray and to exercise their personal faith in God.

A word of caution: Some people put their faith in faith, as expressed by this often-heard comment: "Well, Pastor, it really doesn't matter what you believe just as long as you have faith." It does matter what one believes. For Christians today, God expects us to place our faith, trust, and belief in Jesus Christ. When you analyze all of the healing stories in the four Gospels, faith in God to help and heal is present in each story.

Sometimes it is the faith of friends surrounding the one who needs healing. Sometimes it is the faith of the sick person. Sometimes it is the faith of Jesus in his Heavenly Father to bless and heal the sick one. In today's churches, this compassionate, healing faith could be expressed by a prayer team, a pastor, a prayer chain, or by persons who sit quietly in the pews, praying faithfully and fervently.

Let us revisit these five healing stories as recorded in the Gospels. Who can identify the faith factor in each story? (*Invite brief discussion around each scripture passage.*)

- In the healing of the leper (Matthew 8:1-4)?
- In the healing of the Roman soldier's servant (Matthew 8:5-13)?
- In the healing of Peter's mother-in-law (Matthew 8:14-15)?
- In the healing of the woman with a flow of blood (Matthew 9:20-22)?
- In the healing of the paralyzed man (Mark 2:1-5,11-12)?

Do you get the picture? Faith in God connects with the spiritual dimension in the healing process. The faith-factor is always present in personal healings in Biblical times. So, back to our opening question: Does faith heal? Yes, but not faith-in-faith. Rather, for the Christian it is faith in the healing Christ who loves each one of us and wants abundant, healthy lives for all of us. The role of faith is crucial; and the more we exercise our personal faith, the better the results. Amen.

Prayers for Others

Now let us bring to the Healing Christ
on the stretchers of our prayers

and on the wings of our faith
those loved ones and friends, not present in this room,
    but very much in our thoughts and on our hearts.
(Invite the congregation to pray silently. Do not rush.)

Prayer of Intercession

**God of compassion, source of life and health:
strengthen, relieve, and restore your daughters and sons
whom we have named in our hearts
and lifted into the light and love of Jesus.
May those for whom we pray find health
and experience a renewed confidence in your loving care.
We pray through him who healed the sick,
the physician of our souls, even Jesus Christ our Lord.
    Amen.**

(The Book of Common Prayer; alt. by Laurence Hull Stookey.
Alt. © 1989 The United Methodist Publishing House as published in *The United Methodist Hymnal,* 457)

The Peace

Let us as God's forgiven and accepted people offer one another
signs of reconciliation and love.

Hymn

- "Healer of Our Every Ill," by Marty Haugen
- "There's Something About That Name," by Gloria
  Gaither and William J. Gaither

The Sacrament of Holy Communion

Prayers for Healing the Body, Mind,
Spirit, and Relationships

You are invited to come forward for personal prayer for yourself
or on behalf of another person. You may express your concern to

the prayer team who will anoint you with oil, make the sign of the cross on your forehead, and gently lay on hands with prayer.

Sharing Our Thanksgivings and Blessings

Closing Hymn
- "Give Thanks," by Henry Smith
- "Lord, Dismiss Us with Thy Blessing," attributed to John Fawcett

Dismissal Prayer and Sending Forth
And now let us believe in our hearts
   the words that we have said and sung;
and what we believe in our hearts,
   may we live in our lives, for the glory of God
   this day and evermore. Amen.

CHAPTER TEN

FORGIVENESS AND HEALING

B roken relationships can be more difficult to heal than physical illnesses. Unforgiving attitudes and actions, resentment and bitterness, hurtful and harmful situations: all
these forgiveness and unforgiveness issues are encompassed in the
healing ministry. The following service of healing may evoke
painful memories and touch sensitive areas of our common life
together, but it also offers an effective spiritual therapy in the
healing process.

Gathering (with Music or in Silence)

Welcome and Announcements

Introduction

The focus of our worship service today is forgiveness in healing
ourselves and healing our relationships with others. Christians
are expected to be forgiving people, as lived and taught by Jesus.
Yet, forgiveness is not easy to do every time someone hurts us in
any way. We may find ourselves asking the same question Peter
asked Jesus:

Lord, . . . how often should I forgive? As many as seven times?
(Matthew 18:21)

We frequently pray the Lord's Prayer without taking seriously
Jesus' comment on forgiveness immediately following the prayer:

> For if you forgive others their trespasses, your heavenly Father
> will also forgive you; but if you do not forgive others, neither
> will your Father forgive your trespasses. (Matthew 6:14-15)

So we gather here today not only to receive God's gift of forgiveness for ourselves, but also to call on God's help in giving the gift
of forgiveness to others.

Call to Worship (from Psalms 25:4-5; 86:5; 130:4)

Make me to know your ways, O LORD;
Teach me your paths.
Lead me in your truth, and teach me,
For you are the God of my salvation.
For you, O Lord, are good and forgiving,
Abounding in steadfast love to all who call on you.
There is forgiveness with you,
So that you may be revered.

The Lord's Prayer (Ecumenical Version)

Our Father in heaven,
hallowed be your name,
your kingdom come,
your will be done, on earth as in heaven.
Give us this day our daily bread.
Forgive us our sins
as we forgive those who sin against us.
Save us from the time of trial
and deliver us from evil.
For the kingdom, the power, and the glory are yours
now and forever. Amen.

Hymn

- "Pass Me Not, O Gentle Savior," by Fanny J. Crosby
- "There Is a Balm in Gilead," African-American Spiritual

Holy Scripture Reading

- Luke 7:36-50

Message: "The Jesus Way of Forgiveness"

The Kingdom of God is based on maintaining right relationships with God and with other human beings. Jesus knew that his followers would abuse, misuse, fracture, and break the delicate bonds that connect one with another. This is why Jesus frequently addressed the importance of forgiveness and modeled a forgiveness lifestyle throughout his earthly ministry. Because forgiveness is contrary to our basic human nature, we look to Jesus to guide us and motivate us.

Come once more to Simon's dinner party, as recorded in Luke 7:36-50. Be sensitive to the Jesus way of forgiveness. Why do you suppose that Simon, a highly respected Pharisee and community leader, invited Jesus, along with a few select friends, into his home for dinner? As the story unfolds it is obvious that Simon had no desire to know Jesus as his Messiah. Simon simply thought that Jesus would be an interesting conversation piece for his friends.

However, these curiosity-seekers were more than a bit shaken up when an uninvited guest made her appearance and began to give her full attention to Jesus. Mideastern hospitality dictated certain courtesies for invited guests. The host was expected to provide water and towels to wash and dry dusty feet. Also, a kiss-of-peace greeting and placing drops of sweet-smelling perfume on the heads of the guests would be the customary order of the day. Simon offered Jesus none of these gracious gestures; whereas, this woman, who remains nameless in the story, but is identified as a sinner with a shady reputation, not only crashed the dinner party but proceeded boldly to lavish upon Jesus what Simon had overlooked or ignored, perhaps intentionally.

All this infuriated Simon. With his dinner party totally disrupted, he interpreted Jesus' acceptance of the woman's actions as proof that he was not from God, otherwise Jesus would have known all about her sinful past and would not have allowed her to touch him. Jesus decided to confront Simon.

Notice what Jesus did not do. He did not attempt a quick fix in an embarrassing situation. Jesus, as he often did, seized the opportunity to engage in some teaching moments with Simon and his guests.

First he told Simon a short story (parable) about canceling debts and mending relationships. Then to help Simon fully understand, Jesus turned to the woman, praising her for her non-verbal, yet clear signs of appreciation and respect.

Jesus proceeded to bring it all together by announcing to everyone in the room: "Furthermore, this dear woman, though her past sins were many, has been forgiven, and has made a new beginning in her life. This is why she came here today expressing her heartfelt gratitude." Turning to Simon, Jesus continued, "But the one to whom little is forgiven, loves little." Addressing the woman, Jesus said, "Your sins are forgiven. Your faith has saved you; go in peace" (from Luke 7:47-50).

Several learnings begin to emerge from this story of the uninvited, forgiven guest:

- Jesus took the initiative and did not wait for all involved parties to agree to be more agreeable.
- Jesus confronted the issues, the hurt, the problem while attempting to rebuild and reconcile relationships.
- Jesus offered total forgiveness and the opportunity to start over, to begin a new life without being stuck in the past.

Did Simon have a change of heart? What happened to the woman after that dramatic scene? What about the other dinner guests? Did Jesus have an impact on their attitudes and actions? Only God knows. What we do know is that this story clearly demonstrates the Jesus way of forgiveness.

With God's help and by God's grace, we too can take the initiative in resolving difficult issues among those we love and care about, as well as neighbors and strangers; we too can make attempts to reconcile fractured relationships; we too can offer forgiveness to others and the opportunity to start over. The Jesus way of forgiveness is intended to be the way of forgiveness for everyone who has been baptized into the body of Christ, the church, and who desires to live and to grow in the mind and spirit of Christ.

Silent Reflection

A Guided Prayer of Forgiveness

(Invite the congregation to breathe deeply, to relax the mind and the body, to get as comfortable as possible; to be open and receptive to God's grace and mercy during this guided meditation.)

We adore you, O Christ. We praise you, O Christ, because through your holy cross you have redeemed the world and saved each of us from our sins. Yes, through your holy cross you have forgiven us and loved us even before we know what forgiveness and love were all about. *(Pause.)*

Right now, O Christ, each one of us comes to you seeking help in being a forgiving person. *(Pause.)*

Some of us are having difficulty in forgiving. We need your strength and the willingness to forgive. Help each of us overcome stubbornness and pride that cripple us in so many ways. *(Pause.)*

And now, O Christ, in a conscious, deliberate act of our will, we want to forgive everyone who has anything against any of us.

Some of us need to forgive our parents. *(Pause.)*

Some of us need to forgive our children. *(Pause.)*

Some of us need to forgive God, our heavenly Lord. *(Pause.)*

Some of us need to forgive ourselves. *(Pause.)*

Some of us need to forgive someone who died before we were reconciled. *(Pause.)*

Lord, hear our prayers as we pray specifically by name for others whom we need to forgive. *(Pause.)*

We now give to you all those persons we have named in forgiveness as well as ourselves. As you direct any of us to take tangible action, give us the will to follow through with a phone call, a personal letter, an apology, or restitution. *(Pause.)*

Gracious, merciful Lord, help each one of us know the joy of forgiveness; the joy of burdens taken away; the joy of new life in Christ; the joy of health and wholeness in body, mind, spirit, and in all relationships. In the name of the Father, the Son, and the Holy Spirit we pray and dedicate ourselves. Amen.

(Adapted from *Blessed to Be a Blessing*, copyright © 1980 by James K. Wagner and The Upper Room®, 88–89. Used by permission of Upper Room Books®, http://www.bookstore.upper room.org, 1-800-972-0433.)

Hymn

- "Heal Me, Hands of Jesus," by Michael Perry
- "I Love You, Lord," by Laurie Klein

Holy Communion (optional)

Personal Prayers for Healing the Body, Mind, Spirit, and Relationships

(Read James 5:14-16.) You are invited to come forward to one of the prayer teams for any personal need or on behalf of another person. Receive the anointing oil and the gentle laying on of hands in the name of Jesus Christ who freely offers us forgiveness and healing, new life, and inner peace.

Closing Prayer

As we bask in the sunshine of your grace, remind us, Merciful God, and help us, Patient God, to be more faithful and more consistent in forgiving others as you forgive us. As your son Jesus freely forgave, blessed, and healed, so we desire to freely give to others what we have been given by Jesus. In his holy name we pray. Amen.

Hymn

- "Go Now in Peace," by Natalie Sleeth
- "Shalom to You," traditional Hebrew blessing; translated by Robert N. Deschner

Blessing and Dismissal

Go now in peace, for the Peace of Christ goes with you. Amen.

CHAPTER ELEVEN

A SILENT PRAYER SERVICE

This healing service, using the silent method of praying for and with others, is adapted from a service originally developed at the Mount Washington United Methodist Church in Baltimore, Maryland. For many years, on Thursdays at 11:00 a.m., people gathered in the sanctuary for fifty to sixty minutes. The liturgy was announced as the service progressed. Holy Communion was not offered. Anointing oil was optional. The same hymn was sung every week. Over the years this uncomplicated, simple prayer service touched, helped, and healed countless numbers of people. Use this liturgy as is or adapt it to be more effective for your needs and setting (also see Wagner, *An Adventure in Healing and Wholeness*, 138).

Greetings, Welcome, Announcements

Hymn
- "Breathe on Me, Breath of God," by Edwin Hatch

Scripture Reading
- Luke 5:17-26

Message (brief)

(Luke 5:17-26 is one of the most heartwarming healing stories in the New Testament, with several layers to explore. Consider the following teaching themes that could be developed.)

- The popularity of Jesus—"They had come from every village of Galilee and Judea and from Jerusalem" (v. 17). The houses were too small for the crowds.
- Jesus had the power to heal—Notice that power came from God. Jesus always gave credit to his Heavenly Father (v. 17). When someone is helped or healed because of something we do, do we give God the credit?
- The stretcher-bearers were truly faithful friends to the paralyzed man. They were bold enough to bring him to Jesus for healing, even making a hole in the roof large enough to let him down into the room (v. 19). Do we have the same determination and creativity in bringing our friends to Jesus?
- Luke records Jesus' observation with a profound statement: "When Jesus saw their faith, he said, 'Friend, your sins are forgiven (v. 20) . . . stand up and take your bed and go to your home'" (v. 24). What is the role of faith in the healing process? Did the man who was healed have faith in Jesus? His friends did.
- The paralyzed man never spoke a word in this story. We know nothing about his faith or background. This is an encouraging lesson for intercessory prayer groups in our churches today, who bring people (friends, family, and strangers alike) to the Healing Christ.
- Jesus forgave the man's sins as a significant step in the overall healing. This led to a heated discussion between Jesus and the religious leaders (v. 22-24). What is the connection between sin and sickness? Is all illness caused by sin? Name some sinful habits and behaviors that result in ill health. Name some illnesses that may not be brought on by sin.
- The man who was healed went home glorifying God (v. 25) and all the people in the room glorified God

(v. 26). What are some ways we can glorify God today? Unpack the meaning of "glory" and "glorify."

Pastoral Prayer

Compassionate and Healing God, we thank you for faithful friends in churches everywhere, who consistently care enough to give of their energy, time, and resources to bring on the stretchers of their prayers countless numbers of human beings (friends and strangers alike) who truly need your loving, health-giving Presence. We are also thankful for the marvelous ways in which you have created our bodies to heal themselves and we are grateful for all who minister your healing in the healthcare professions. As we come to you now for the healing touch of your Son, Jesus Christ, we affirm the unity of body, mind, and spirit. Restore to each of us harmony, balance, and health, that we may serve and glorify you this day and in all the days ahead. Amen.

Intercessory Prayer

(Persons write prayer concerns on small cards, which are brought forward by an usher and placed on the altar. After a time of silent intercession, the minister prays over the cards, thanking God in advance for healing and wholeness.)

Invitation to Come to the Chancel Railing for Prayers

(Four robed persons—lay and clergy—pray individually with those who come forward, laying on hands with silent prayer. Organ music plays quietly in the background.)

Concluding Statement

(Invite all to come to the parish hall for refreshments and fellowship.)

Benediction

Go forth in peace.
The grace of the Lord Jesus Christ, the love of God,
And the communion of the Holy Spirit be with you all.
Amen.

CHAPTER TWELVE

FOR A HOSPITAL SETTING

The Pastor can bring comfort and offer a special blessing to those in the hospital with a brief service of anointing oil and laying on of hands with prayer. Holy Communion is an option depending on the situation.

Preparation

Bring a small container of oil, usually olive oil. Highly aromatic oils are not recommended because of possible allergic reactions. An introductory word of explanation would be appropriate for those who are not familiar with this ministry. Because Christ instructed his disciples to anoint the sick with oil, the church continues this tradition. The oil does not do the healing; rather, it is an authentic biblical symbol for healing, pointing beyond itself to the presence and compassion of Christ. We anoint with oil not only for physical needs, but also for the healing of emotions, memories, and relationships. Invite all who are present in the room to participate and join with the Pastor in ministering to the patient/parishioner.

This service includes material adapted from *Pastoral Prayers for the Hospital Visit* by Sara Webb Phillips (Nashville: Abingdon Press, 2006), 77–78. It is used by permission.

Invitation

We have come to lift up each other before the Lord,
　especially *(Names)*, that all might receive healing and
　wholeness.

Prayer

Almighty and everlasting God,
who can banish all affliction both of soul and body,
show forth your power upon those in need,
that by your mercy they may be restored to serve you afresh
in holiness of living, through Jesus Christ our Lord. Amen.

Holy Scripture Reading

(Choose from among the following passages.)

- Psalm 23
- Matthew 11:28-30
- Romans 12:9-18
- Philippians 4:6-8

Pastoral Prayer over the Oil (optional)

O God, the giver of health and salvation,
　we give thanks to you for the gift of oil.
As your holy apostles anointed many who were sick and
　healed them,
　　so pour your Holy Spirit on us and on this gift,
　that those who in faith and repentance receive this anoint-
　　ing may be made whole;
through Jesus Christ our Lord. **Amen.**

*(The Book of Common Prayer, 1979, alt. as published in The
United Methodist Book of Worship, 620)*

Anointing with Oil

*(The pastor anoints the patient and others who are open to being
anointed. Making the sign of the cross on the forehead, the pastor
says:)*

(*Name*), I anoint you with oil in the name of the Father, and of the Son, and of the Holy Spirit.

Laying on of Hands
(*All are then invited to join hands or gently touch the patient as the pastor prays.*)
May the power of God's indwelling presence
   heal you of all illnesses of body, mind, spirit, and relationships
that you may serve God with a loving heart. Amen.

Personal Prayers (optional)
(*The pastor, the patient, and others in the room may want to express personal prayers. Highest consideration is always given to the patient's condition. Be brief and be sensitive to the time.*)

Holy Communion (optional)

Prayer after Anointing and Laying on of Hands
Gracious and loving God,
   we truly thank you for your gifts of healing today.
We continue to pray
that you will comfort each of us in our suffering,
that you will grant us your strength when we are weak,
that you will bless us with your patience
   when we are anxious,
that you will be very close when we are alone and lonely,
that you will bring us hope and encouragement
   when we are discouraged and afraid,
(*if appropriate*) and when death comes,
   you will open your arms to receive (*Name*).
In the name of Jesus Christ we pray as he taught us:
Our Father who art in heaven . . .

Blessing
Now may the peace of God that surpasses all human
   understanding
   guard our hearts and minds in Christ Jesus. Amen.

FOR A CONGREGATION IN CONFLICT

When the body of Christ is so divided over certain issues that negative attitudes and pessimism prevail, when factions within a congregation are at an impasse without agreeable solutions, consider a healing service designed to encourage reconciliation, to focus on the forgiving grace of Christ, and to restore harmony. Our role in the church is not to impose change on anyone, but rather to love one another, as Christ taught us. God's role is to do the changing. Only God can bring a healing transformation out of contentious circumstances. Because of the multi-layered issues that surround and influence a congregation struggling with discord, the pastor and the healing ministry planning team need to proceed with prayer, sensitivity, and nonjudgmental attitudes.

The following healing service is not designed for the Sunday morning worship hour. It would be more helpful with a smaller group such as the church council/official board or a gathering of those who respond to an open invitation. This liturgy can be revised and adapted to be more effective in your situation. To encourage dialog and openness, meet in a room with tables and chairs arranged in a circle. Have notepaper, pens/pencils, and Bibles on each table. In the center of the circle place a smaller table with a lit candle, a loaf of bread, and a chalice of grape juice. The candle symbolizes the light and presence of Christ.

The Gathering

(Have quiet, meditative music in the background. Use of recorded music allows the church musicians to participate more fully in the healing service, except to accompany hymn singing.)

Welcome and Greeting

(Offered by the pastor or a lay leader)
In the Name of our Lord and Savior Jesus Christ, the one who has called us into his Church, and by whose amazing grace we have life, health, and salvation, I welcome each one of you. As we come together to experience the healing presence of Christ among us, let us remember that our role in the church is not to change each other, but to love one another, as Christ taught us. God's role is to change hearts, attitudes, and behavior. "Here we enter a fellowship; sometimes we will agree to differ; always we will resolve to love; and unite to serve" (ascribed to E. Stanley Jones).

Opening Prayer

Gracious and loving God, we know within our heart of hearts that you accept and love each of us just as we are and that we can never do anything that will cause you to love us less or more than you do today. Yet, we also know that you love us too much to allow us to stay the way we are and that beginning at our baptism, your goal is for each of us to become new creations in Christ, however long that takes. Therefore, we come asking you to help us maintain the unity of the Spirit, to experience the forgiving grace of Christ, and to restore understanding, love, and harmony within each of us, within our church, and within our world. All this we offer to you in the name of Jesus Christ our Lord. Amen.

Hymn or Chorus

- "Help Us Accept Each Other," by Fred Kahn
- "People Need the Lord," by Greg Nelson and Phill McHugh

Holy Scripture Readings

- John 17:1-11
- Ephesians 4:1-6

Silent Reflection

Message (brief)

The history of the Christian movement from the time of Christ to this very day records numerous footnotes describing congregations in conflict. These could range from theological issues to deciding church leadership to dealing with outside forces or to resolving personal differences. Because of basic human nature, free will, personal motivations and ambitions, conflict among Christians cannot be avoided. Yet, some followers of Christ have the unrealistic expectation that walking into a church building ought to be something like experiencing a bit of heaven on earth, where love, peace, and harmony prevail every day in every way.

Recall that even Jesus had to deal with disharmony among his twelve apostles. The first major argument in the New Testament era occurred when Peter and the leaders of the Jerusalem church clashed over the criteria to follow in accepting converts to the Christian faith. Some insisted converts had to follow Jewish rituals and laws; others opposed this position. Several of Paul's letters to the early churches chronicle strife and stress within congregations.

Question: Is it possible to be faithful to Christ, to the gospel, and to the purpose and mission of the church without achieving one hundred percent agreement and harmony among all church members?

Answer: Yes, yes, yes! Healthy, growing, maturing congregations agree to disagree, to respect each other's differing opinions and experiences, but also to employ the guiding counsel of the apostle Paul in Ephesians 4:2-3: "with all humility and gentleness, with patience, bearing with one another in love, making every effort to maintain the unity of the Spirit in the bond of peace."

As our discussions, feelings, and thoughts begin to unfold during our time together, let us hold as our highest value and most precious gift, the love that our Lord Jesus Christ has for each of us. Whatever may divide us, let us claim and live the prayer Jesus prayed for his followers, as recorded in John 17:11, "Holy Father, protect them in your name, that you have given me, so that they may be one, as we are one."

Discerning God's Will for Our Church

Introduction

Discernment is the process by which we seek God's will so that we may know what to pray for and what action we are to take. In discernment we assume that the God who loves us passionately also yearns to communicate with us. Although we may encounter our own static, we trust that God is able to get through to us somehow in times of discernment. This discernment process is based on and adapted from *Stretch Out Your Hand Leader's Guide: Exploring Healing Prayer* copyright© by Tilda Norbreg and Robert D. Webber, 38–40. It is used by permission of Upper Room Books, www.bookstore.upperroom.org, 1-800-972-0433.

Reflection Statements to be Read Aloud

Our faith and belief includes:

- (*Name of Our Church*) is called by God to be faithful to Jesus Christ by welcoming new people into the church, by proclaiming and teaching the gospel, by healing brokenness and disease, by making disciples, and by agreeing to disagree, yet resolving to love as we unite to serve. (*Pause.*)
- God knows what we need and is able to give us even "more than we can ask or think." Jesus taught us to come to God with our problems, as a child would come to a parent. (*Pause.*)
- God uses our personal energies, talents, and commitment. We are invited to engage fully in what God might be doing among us, in us, and through us. (*Pause.*)

- Surrendering to God's will is not so much "giving up" as "giving over" all things into God's hands. (*Pause.*)
- The faith to move mountains is not so much our trusting that a certain thing will happen as trusting in God to work lovingly and creatively in our problems. (*Pause.*)
- We seek God's will in our particular situation and pray for God's way to be made known. This may mean putting aside our personal agendas and being open to surprising new direction. (*Pause.*)

Invite the group to share their reactions and comments to these statements of faith and belief. Politely resist any effort to offer solutions and action plans at this time. Assure them that there will be opportunity to suggest positive next steps later.

Following the discussion time, check with the group about taking a short break or going on.

Listening and Praying

Now let us come to God and tell God as honestly as we can what we believe we really need and how we feel about this need. Be honest here, admitting feelings of worry, hopelessness, confusion, anger, and so on. You may want to write down anything that comes to you. (*Pause.*)

- Invite God to enter into our problem. Try to put into one sentence the main issue of contention. Jesus instructed us that if we ask, seek, and knock, we would be given what we ask, find what we seek, and the door would open. Release to God the problem as you understand it. (*Pause.*)
- Now silently sit in God's presence. Try to stop talking in your own head. Be still, listen, expect God to communicate and begin working in some way. (*Pause.*)
- Pay attention to what happens next within you: images, thoughts, memories, verses of scripture, physical sensations, action steps, and the like. For now trust that whatever emerges does so for a reason related to the issue at hand. (*Pause.*)

Writing and Sharing

Next, write down in just a few words what came to you. Then share with the group what each of you sensed in your personal discernment. (*Provide time for sharing and discussion.*)

Is there an emerging direction for the group? Yes . . . no . . . maybe? We may need to have more sessions of group discernment after today. I urge each of us to continue the discernment process in our private prayers when we are alone with God. Continue to give the situation over to God and listen for the Holy Spirit's movements. Keep in mind that the church belongs to Christ, who is the Foundation and the Head, and who promised, "Remember, I am with you."

Take time for a brief break (if needed)

Hymn or Chorus
- "Heal Us, Emmanuel, Hear Our Prayer," by William Cowper
- "Spirit of the Living God," by Daniel Iverson

Confession and Assurance of Pardon

As we prepare to come to the Lord's Table in Holy Communion let us join in moments of confession. Let us pray:

Almighty and all-loving God, through your Son Jesus Christ
    you have reconciled the world to yourself.
Help us now to be reconciled with one another,
    that again we might dwell in the warmth of your love.
Inspire us with your Holy Spirit
    to put aside the cloak of pride and put on Christ,
    that we might forgive and be forgiven;
        through Jesus Christ our Lord. Amen.
(*Moments of Silent Confession*)

(Michael J. O'Donnell, [© 1992 UMPH] in *The United Methodist Book of Worship*, 489)

Assurance of Pardon

Receive the good news: Christ died and rose for each of us,
    proving God's love and forgiveness.

In the name of Jesus Christ you are forgiven.
In the name of Jesus Christ you are forgiven.
Thanks be to God. Amen!

Form a Circle and Pass the Peace of Christ

The Holy Communion

(The pastor offers the prayer of thanksgiving, words of institution, and invites all to pray the Lord's Prayer. After breaking the loaf of bread, the pastor will start the bread and the cup around the circle. Use the intinction method: take a piece of bread and dip it into the cup. An effective method for serving communion in a circle is to serve to the left and pass to the right. This avoids the awkwardness of serving with a mouthful of bread. It also adds the gracious element of each person serving before they are served. After all have been served, join hands for a moment of silent reflection. Then invite informal sharing of what this time together has meant.)

Closing Hymn

- "Amazing Grace," by John Newton
- "Blest Be The Tie That Binds," by John Fawcett

Closing Prayer

Healing and Reconciling God, as we come to the close of our time together today, we turn to you one more time, knowing that only you can change hearts, inner attitudes, and desires. Therefore, we leave that gracious, healing ministry to you. However, as we have been blessed in coming to your Son Jesus at his Communion Table, so may we now bless one another with a renewed effort to keep working on our differences, and to love each other, as we love ourselves. Amen.

Sending Forth

May we believe in our hearts the words that we have said, and sung, and written; and what we believe in our hearts, may we live in our lives, to the glory of Christ and the church. Go in peace. Amen.

CHAPTER FOURTEEN

FOLLOWING CONGREGATIONAL TRAUMA OR TRAGEDY

Trauma and tragedy too often accompany the consequences of fires, floods, hurricanes, tornadoes, earthquakes, violence, and vandalism. These uncontrollable, outside forces can have a devastating impact on the members and friends of the congregation. This healing service is designed to help one another get in touch with the comforting, supporting, encouraging grace of God in the midst of severe loss and grief.

Because words are often inadequate to express the inexpressible, allow time to be quiet, reflective, and meditative. The sacrament of Holy Communion, with its main focus on the presence of the risen Christ, can be an effective spiritual therapy. Let music, scriptures, prayers, silence, sacrament, and symbols of the faith connect with the congregation.

Gathering and Centering
(If music is played, let it be quiet and relaxing. Gathering in silence may be the most appropriate way to begin.)

Personal Meditation upon Entering the Sanctuary

God, grant me
> the serenity to accept the things I cannot change,
> the courage to change the things I can,
> and the wisdom to distinguish one from the other. Amen.
> (Anonymous, *The United Methodist Hymnal*, 459)

Welcome and Greeting

(Make announcements and give instructions regarding this healing service.)

Call to Worship (based on Psalm 30:5, 10-12)

Weeping may tarry for the night,
But joy comes with the morning.
Hear, O Lord, and be gracious to us.
O Lord, be our helper.
For you, O Lord, have turned our mourning into dancing;
You have clothed us with gladness.
So that we may praise you and not be silent.
O Lord, our god, we give thanks to you forever.

Praise Hymns

- "Because He Lives," by Gloria and William J. Gaither
- "Kum Ba Ya (Come By Here)," African American Spiritual
- "O Christ, the Healer," by Fred Pratt Green

Opening Prayer

O God, whose grace and mercy flow like an endless river, help each one of us place ourselves in the path of your boundless love and limitless compassion. May we find our spirits renewed, our bodies healed, our minds cleared, and our hearts overflowing with love, forgiveness, and grace. In Jesus' name we pray and gather in this place. Amen.

Holy Scripture Readings
(*Choose one of the following passages:*)

- 1 Kings 19:11-12
- Psalm 130
- Psalm 131
- Matthew 11:28-30
- Romans 8:26-28
- 2 Corinthians 1:2-4
- Philippians 4:6-8

Message of Healing and Hope
(*The homilist will be very sensitive to specific hurts and losses, speaking from a pastoral heart and a compassionate spirit. It is not helpful to dwell on the unanswerable question, "Why did this happen to us?" Rather, move in a more positive direction with these questions:*)

- Now that this has happened, what might we do next?
- What could be our next steps?
- Where do we see God leading us from here?
- What is God providing for our reconstruction, renewal, and resurrection?

Response to the Word
- Receive an Offering (perhaps to assist in financial recovery)
- Special Music (perhaps a timely and suitable vocal solo)

Prayers for Others
(*Invite informal sharing of names and situations or ask these to be written on cards and brought forward by the ushers.*)

Prayer Hymn
- "Lord, Listen to Your Children Praying," by Ken Medema

Intercessory Prayer

God of compassion, source of life and health:
strengthen, relieve, and restore your daughters and sons
whom we have named in our hearts
and lifted into the light and love of Jesus.
May those for whom we pray find health
and experience a renewed confidence in your loving care.
We pray through him who healed the sick,
the physician of our souls, even Jesus Christ our Lord. Amen.

(*The Book of Common Prayer*; alt. by Laurence Hull Stookey.
Alt. © 1989 The United Methodist Publishing House as published in *The United Methodist Hymnal*, 457)

Confession of Sin and Assurance of Pardon

We are reluctant, O Author of Love,
to set aside our hurt, our anger, our disappointment.
Heal us with your tender touch,
that we might be cleansed of all unclean thoughts,
all schemes of revenge, all hope of vindictive retribution.
Open our eyes to the power of love,
shown to us in the unselfish sacrifice
of your Son, our Savior, Jesus Christ. Amen.

(Michael J. O'Donnell [© 1992 UMPH] in *The United Methodist
Book of Worship*, 491)

(All offer prayers of confession in silence.)

If we confess our sins,
God who is faithful and just will forgive us our sins
and cleanse us from all unrighteousness (1 John 1:9).
The almighty and merciful Lord, grant [us] . . . remission of all
our sins,
true repentance, amendment of life,
and the grace and consolation of [the] Holy Spirit. Amen.

(*The Book of Common Prayer*, 1928, 24)

The Peace of Christ

Let us offer one another signs of reconciliation and love.

Hymn of Preparation

- "Turn Your Eyes upon Jesus," by Helen H. Lemmel
- "Stand By Me," by Charles Albert Tindley

Sacrament of Holy Communion

(For Great Thanksgiving Prayers consult your denominational worship resources or any of the following:)

- *The United Methodist Book of Worship* (Nashville: The United Methodist Publishing House, 1992), 33–80.
- *The United Methodist Hymnal* (Nashville: The United Methodist Publishing House, 1989), 2–31.
- *Communion Services*, by Robin Knowles Wallace (Nashville: Abingdon Press, 2006), 87.

The Lord's Prayer

Prayers for Personal Healing of Body, Mind, Spirit, and Relationships

(Have quiet music playing in the background as the worshipers come forward for anointing with oil and laying on of hands with prayer. Invite people to come for themselves or on behalf of others.)

Closing Prayer

Eternal God, we give you thanks for this holy mystery
    in which you have given yourself to us.
Grant that we may go into the world
    in the strength of your Spirit,
    to give ourselves for others,
in the name of Jesus Christ our Lord. Amen.

(From *A Service of Word and Table I*, copyright 1972, 1980, 1985, 1989 The United Methodist Publishing House, as published in *The United Methodist Hymnal*, 11)

Hymn of Dedication
- "He Touched Me," by William J. Gaither
- "Hymn of Promise," by Natalie Sleeth
- "This Is a Day of New Beginnings," by Brian Wren

Benediction (Romans 15:13)
May the God of hope
   fill you with all joy and peace in believing,
so that you may abound in hope
   by the power of the Holy Spirit. Amen and Amen!

Congregational Response
- "On Eagle's Wings," by Michael Joncas

BIBLICAL HEALING PASSAGES

Individual Healings by Jesus

Description	Matthew	Mark	Luke	John
Nobleman's son				4:46-54
Unclean spirit		1:21-29	4:31-37	
Simon's mother-in-law	8:14-15	1:29-31	4:38-39	
A leper	8:1-4	1:4-45	5:12-16	
Paralytic carried by four	9:1-9	2:1-12	5:17-26	
Sick man at the pool				5:2-18
Withered hand	12:9-14	3:1-6	6:6-11	
Centurion's servant	8:5-13		7:2-10	
Widow's son raised			7:11-17	
Demoniac(s) at Gadara	8:28-34	5:1-20	8:26-36	
Issue of blood	9:20-22	5:25-34	8:43-48	
Jairus's daughter raised	9:18-26	5:21-43	8:40-56	
Two blind men	9:27-31			
Dumb devil possessed	9:32-34			
Daughter of Canaan woman	15:21-28	7:24-30		
Deaf, speech impediment		7:32-37		
Blind man of Bethsaida		8:22-26		
Epileptic boy	17:14-21	9:14-29	9:37-42	
Man born blind				9:1-14
Raising of Lazarus				11:1-44
Ten lepers			17:11-19	
Blind Bartimaeus	20:29-34	10:45-52	18:35-43	

Multiple Healings by Jesus

	Matthew	Mark	Luke	John
Crowd at Peter's door	8:6-17	1:32-34	4:40-41	
Crowds after leper healed			5:14-16	
Crowd near Capernaum	12:15-21	3:7-12	5:17-19	
Answering John's question	11:2-6		7:18-23	
Before feeding the 5,000	14:13-14		9:11	
Crowds beyond the Jordan	19:1-2			
Blind & lame in temple	21:14			
Some sick of Nazareth	13:53-58	6:1-6		
All kinds of sickness	4:23	6:56		
Every sickness & disease	9:35			
All oppressed (Acts 10:38)				

Individual Healings by the Apostles

Description	Acts
The lame man from birth	3:1-12
Paul regains his sight	3:10-22; 22:11-13
Aeneas the paralytic	9:32-35
Raising of Dorcas	9:36-42
Crippled man by Lystra	14:8-18
Girl with a spirit of divination	16:16-18
Eutychus restored to life	20:7-12
Paul healed of snakebite	28:1-6
Father of Publius healed	28:7-8

Multiple Healings by the Apostles

Description	Acts
Many wonders and signs	2:43
Many sick healed in Jerusalem	5:12-16
Stephen performs many miracles	6:8
Philip heals many at Samaria	8:5-13
Paul and Barnabas work signs and wonders	14:3
Paul heals at Ephesus	19:11-12
Sick healed at Melita	28:9

Other New Testament Healing Passages

Description	Passage
Anointing	Mark 6:13; James 5:14
Jesus' instructions	
& promises to believers	Mark 16:14-20; Luke 10:8-9
Signs and wonders	Romans 15:18-19; 2 Corinthians 12:12; Hebrews 2:4
Healing	1 Corinthians 12:9; 12:28-30
Perfect eternal healing	Revelations 21:4

Some Old Testament References to Healing

Description	Passage
None of these diseases	Exodus 15:26
The fiery serpent	Numbers 21:6-9
Schunammite's son raised	2 Kings 4:18-37
Naaman healed	2 Kings 5:1-14
Dead man raised	2 Kings 13:20-21
Hezekiah healed	2 Kings 20:1-11
Some healing psalms	Psalms 23; 30; 103
With his stripes we are healed	Isaiah 53:5

Selected Resources

Books

Day, Albert E. *Letters on the Healing Ministry.* Nashville, Tenn.: Upper Room Books, 1986. To obtain copies contact: Disciplined Order of Christ, P.O. Box 753, Ashland, Ohio 44805.

Job, Rueben. *A Guide To Spiritual Discernment.* Nashville, Tenn.: Upper Room Books, 1996.

Joyner, F. Belton Jr. *Pastoral Prayers in Public Places.* Nashville, Tenn.: Abingdon Press, 2006.

Matthews, Dale A. *The Faith Factor.* New York, N.Y.: Viking-Penguin, 1998.

Morris, Danny E. *Yearning to Know God's Will.* Grand Rapids, Mich.: Zondervan, 1996.

Norberg, Tilda and Webber, Robert D. *Stretch Out Your Hand: Exploring Healing Prayer.* Nashville, Tenn.: Upper Room Books, 1998.

Pearson, Mark A. *Christian Healing.* Old Tappan, N.J.: Fleming H. Revell Co., 1990.

Phillips, Sara Webb. *Pastoral Prayers for the Hospital Visit.* Nashville, Tenn.: Abingdon, 2006.

Ramirez, Frank. *Partners in Healing: The Ministry of Anointing.* Lima, Ohio: CSS Publishing, 2005.

Rowlett, Martha Graybeal. *Praying Together: Forming Prayer Ministries in Your Congregation.* Nashville, Tenn.: Upper Room Books, 2002.

United Methodist Book of Worship, The, Nashville, Tenn.: The United Methodist Publishing House, 1992.

Upper Room Worshipbook: Music and Liturgies for Spiritual Formation. Compiled and edited by Elise S. Eslinger. Nashville, Tenn.: Upper Room Books, 2006.

Wagner, James K. *An Adventure in Healing and Wholeness.* Nashville, Tenn.: Upper Room Books, 1993.

———— *Forgiveness: The Jesus Way.* Lima, Ohio: CSS Publishing, 2007.

———— *The Spiritual Heart of Your Health.* Nashville, Tenn.: Upper Room Books, 2002.

Wallace, Robin Knowles. *Communion Services.* Nashville, Tenn.: Abingdon Press, 2006.

Wuellner, Flora S. Enter by the Gate: Jesus' Seven Guidelines When Making Hard Choices. Nashville, Tenn.: Upper Room Books, 2005.

VIDEO

"Is Any Among You Suffering?" Videotape on Anointing with Oil: (16 minutes). Contact Brethren Press, 1451 Dundee Avenue, Elgin, Ill. 60120; phone: 847-742-5100.

CONTINUING EDUCATION OPPORTUNITIES IN HEALING MINISTRY

Christian Healing Ministries, Inc.
P. O. Box 9520, 438 West 67th Street
Jacksonville, Florida 32208
Phone: 904-765-3332
Directors: Francis and Judith MacNutt

The MacNutts offer healing ministry training courses and conferences. They also publish a newsletter containing articles and resources related to healing ministries.

Institute for Christian Renewal
148 Plaistow Road
Plaistow, New Hampshire 03865
Phone: 603-382-0291
Directors: Mark and Mary Pearson

The staff offers training in Christian healing ministries throughout the United States. A newsletter listing helpful information, articles, and resources is also published.

International Order of St. Luke the Physician (OSL)
P. O. Box 13701
San Antonio, Texas 78213
Phone: 210-492-5222

OSL publishes the monthly magazine *Sharing* and sponsors healing ministry missions, retreats, and conferences in the United States and Canada. The organization is thoroughly ecumenical and has many local chapters.

Total Living Center
2221 9th Street SW, P. O. Box 6477
Canton, Ohio 44706
Phone: 330-455-3663
Director: Pastor Don Bartow

In addition to conducting seminars, conferences, and workshops around the world, Don Bartow has written and published a wealth of resources related to local church healing and wholeness ministries from a pastor's experience.

SCRIPTURE INDEX

This index refers to the scripture texts suggested for the healing services throughout this book. Do not be limited to these scriptures when designing liturgies for specific settings and situations.

For a complete listing of healing stories in the New Testament, plus some in the Old Testament, consult the Appendix: Biblical Healing Passages on p. 81.

Music Index

The hymns and choruses listed in these healing services are intended to be helpful suggestions, not rigid recommendations. The creative worship planner will want to explore and offer music that is inspirational and appropriate. Be open to the unfamiliar as well as the familiar. Develop sensitivity to the powerful gift of music in a healing environment.

The selected hymns and choruses listed below are taken from the following three resources and include page references to those resources. They can also be found in other music resources:

- *The United Methodist Hymnal* (UMH), Nashville: The United Methodist Publishing House, 1989.
- *The United Methodist Book of Worship* (BOW), Nashville: The United Methodist Publishing House, 1992.
- *The Faith We Sing* (FWS), Nashville: Abingdon Press, 2000.

COMMUNION LITURGY INDEX

This index refers to the healing services in this book that intentionally incorporate the sacrament of Holy Communion. The sacrament of Holy Communion is a highly recommended option when designing and leading any healing service.